EXQUISITE MINIATURES

IN CROSS STITCH AND OTHER COUNTED THREAD TECHNIQUES

EXQUISITE MINIATURES

IN CROSS STITCH AND OTHER COUNTED THREAD TECHNIQUES

BRENDA KEYES

David & Charles

When some small and perfect thing you happen across,
look upon it with love and wonder.

Françoise Marrell

For my wonderful family

A DAVID & CHARLES BOOK

First published in the UK in 1997

ISBN 0 7153 0435 6

Photography by Jon Stewart
Styling by Barbara Stewart
Book design by Anita Ruddell
Printed in Italy by New Interlitho SpA
for David & Charles
Brunel House   Newton Abbot   Devon

CONTENTS

The Projects

INTRODUCTION

It's a rather strange feature of human nature that we feel an uncontrollable urge to 'Ooo' and 'Ah' over tiny things. Babies, puppies, kittens, day-old chicks – all are wonderful! People are drawn to things in miniature. Perhaps it's the mothering instinct that makes us react in this way; but react we do, and not just to living things. A model railway or tiny doll continue to fascinate long after childhood has been left behind. The skill of the miniaturist is held in awe over that of the landscape painter. The list goes on. Whatever the attraction, I am most definitely party to it and this is the reason for writing this book.

If you have already had a quick look through the book, you will notice that although it is called *Exquisite Miniatures*, the projects are not what you could call minuscule. The title takes a broader view, and you don't have to stitch everything at the size I suggest. Because all the designs in the book are charted, they can be made in any size – much larger or even smaller. The beauty of charted designs is their versatility, and you will see in Workbox, page 17, just how easy it is to enlarge or reduce a design to your own requirements.

The state of your eyesight will play a large part in deciding which fabrics you choose to work with, and whether to work over one thread or two, and so forth. My family have had to put up with the rather strange sight of me with my glasses perched either on the bridge of my nose, or more frequently, balanced on my top lip. I know this is eccentric in the extreme, but as a short-sighted person who finds that it is sometimes possible to see close work a great deal better without glasses, it saves a huge amount of precious time to simply flip them over my nose and rest them on my lip, instead of artfully arranging them on my fringe!

If you wish to work some of the finer pieces in the book, but feel that your eyesight would be placed under too much strain, you could take a less eccentric approach than mine and consider using either a magnifier, or a magnifying light. There are many models to choose from, some with daylight-quality light, so do shop around until you find one which suits you. You will find they can enable you to tackle projects that you would have otherwise been unable to. Also, try to work in daylight and, if possible, outdoors. I know this isn't always practical in our climate, but there is nothing nicer, on a warm day, than to sit in the garden and stitch.

Alternative suggestions for using all of the designs have been offered, just as in all my previous books; but here, enlarging the designs was the main consideration in offering other options, so that the projects can be made up in a range of sizes and scales. The overriding reason for wanting to work a particular design should be that you will enjoy working it. If you follow the advice given, and choose fabric counts to suit your eyesight and ability, I feel confident that you will gain as much pleasure in working any of the designs in the book as I have in creating them.

BRENDA KEYES

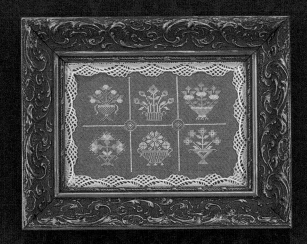

WORKBOX

All the projects in this book, although not all worked in the same stitch, use counted needlework techniques, where the design is worked from a chart rather than being printed on fabric or canvas. The method of reading the chart and then translating it to the fabric is an easy one to master and will open up a host of exciting possibilities. You will be able to work from any counted stitch chart, and will also find it easy to adapt, enlarge, reduce and eventually create designs of your own.

UNDERSTANDING CHARTS

You will come across a wide variety of charts – black and white, hand-drawn, and computer-generated, with coloured squares or symbols, or coloured squares *and* symbols. If the list sounds complicated and daunting, fear not! The method for translating all of them is the same. One square on the chart, containing a symbol or colour, represents one stitch (the instructions for each project will tell you what stitch this is, but most counted needlework is worked in cross stitch). Fig 1 and the picture below show clearly how the chart has been translated on to the fabric.

The blank squares on your chart mean either that this area is unworked or, if you are working on canvas and there is a plain background worked in one colour, instructions will be given as to what colour to use.

Straight black lines surrounding a motif indicate backstitch. They will add impact to your design and will help to define areas that would otherwise blend into each other. Black is usually suggested for outlining but is sometimes too harsh, in which case a softer shade of grey or brown, or any darker shade of a colour already used, is more appropriate.

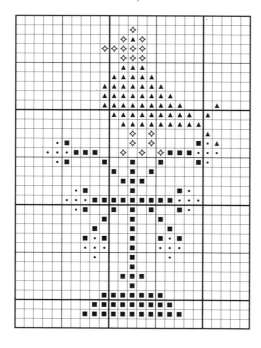

BIRD IN A BUSH MOTIF

DMC STRANDED COTTON (FLOSS)

◇◇	370 olive green	■■	500 dark green
▲▲	300 chocolate brown	••	760 pink

Fig 1 Bird in a bush: The chart and key.

Bird in a bush: The finished embroidery.

Unless the design is worked in one colour only, a key is given to indicate which colours to use for each stitch.

The same motif worked on the same fabric over 1, 2 and 3 threads (top row, left to right) and on rustico and linen (bottom row, left to right).

Counted needlework requires an evenweave fabric: that is, a fabric that has the same number of threads vertically as horizontally. Such fabrics are described by the number of threads or blocks per inch, usually known as the count.

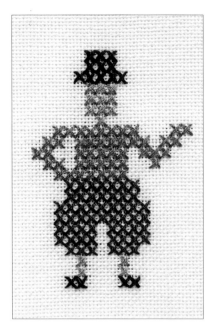

The count determines the finished size of the design. For example, a 25-count fabric has 25 threads per inch; so a design 100 stitches high x 50 wide on this fabric will measure 4 x 2in (10 x 5cm). An 18-count fabric has 18 threads per inch, so the same design worked on this fabric will be 5½ x 2¾in (14 x 7cm).

Most of the designs in this book have been worked on either fine linen, or single thread canvas. Aida fabric (which has threads woven into blocks) has not been used because of the high count needed to produce designs on such a small scale. If you particularly enjoy working on Aida fabric, and find it easier to use, there is really no reason why it cannot be substituted for the fabrics suggested in most of the designs in this book; the finished pieces will just be larger.

I think it's a really good idea to stop and consider your choice of fabric carefully before embarking on any counted needle-work design. Embroidery, as a hobby, should be enjoyable, so choose a fabric that you're comfortable with. Think about changing not only the thread count and type of fabric, but also the colour. On the previous page just some of the many wonderful evenweave fabrics now available to the stitcher are shown, with examples of the results to be achieved by working over one, two or three fabric threads. A little extra thought at the planning stage will ensure that you enjoy working the project as well as admiring it when it is finished.

FABRIC ALLOWANCE

It is important to surround the design area with enough fabric for stretching and framing. Generally, 4–6in (10–15cm) will be sufficient, although smaller pieces, such as brooches and miniatures, will not require this much excess. There is no hard and fast rule because the position of a design and its setting and whether you're going to use a hoop or a frame will influence how much fabric you allow. For example, a brooch could only require a few inches (2.5–5cm) of fabric, even with an allowance for stretching and framing. If you like to work with your fabric held taut in a hoop, however, you would need at least a 6in (15cm) square to fit a 4in (10cm) hoop.

The method for calculating the amount of fabric required for a design (or alternative fabrics with different thread counts) is shown below. Once you have mastered the technique of calculating in this way, you will find it an easy task to select the correct amount of fabric required for counted work.

Always measure your fabric carefully and cut along a thread line using sharp dressmaking scissors. There are a number of methods you can use to prevent the cloth from fraying: oversew the edges by hand; machine the edges using a zig-zag stitch; bind the edges with tape (not masking tape as it can pull threads when being removed and leave a nasty, sticky residue); or use a commercially made material called Fray-check, which is applied to the edges of the fabric.

CALCULATING QUANTITIES OF ALTERNATIVE FABRICS

Cross stitching on linen over two threads

For example: Linen 25 threads per inch (2.5cm) with design area 100 stitches high x 50 wide.

Divide the number of vertical stitches in the design area by the stitch count of the fabric and multiply by two. This will give you the size of the design area in inches (or centimetres). Repeat this procedure for the horizontal stitches.

Thus: $\frac{100}{25}$ = 4 x 2 = 8in (20.5cm)
          $\frac{50}{25}$ = 2 x 2 = 4in (10cm)

So the design area is 8 x 4in (20.5 x 10cm).

Add 4–6in (10–15cm) (or less; see advice in Fabric Allowance), for finishing, and the fabric required is 12 x 8in (30.5 x 20.5cm).

Cross stitching over one thread of linen or on block fabrics such as Aida

For example: 18-count Aida with design area 72 stitches high x 54 wide.

Divide the number of vertical stitches in the design area by the stitch count of the fabric and this will give you the design area in inches (or centimetres). Repeat this procedure for the horizontal stitches.

Thus: $^{72}/_{18}$ = 4in (10cm)
             $^{54}/_{18}$ = 3in (8cm)

So the design area is 4 x 3in (10 x 8cm).

Add 4–6in (10–15cm) (or less; see advice in Fabric Allowance), for finishing, and the fabric required is 8 x 7in (20.5 x 18cm).

THREADS

The vast range of threads available, in an enormous choice of colours, offers the stitcher almost unlimited design possibilities. The most commonly used thread for counted needlework is stranded cotton (floss). The advantage of stranded cotton (floss) is that it can be separated out and any number or colour combination of strands recombined to achieve different effects and to enable it to be used on a number of different fabrics. As the cotton (floss) has six strands, many variations are possible. Two strands are commonly used for cross stitch on a fairly fine linen or Aida, although one strand can be used over one thread of linen to create delicate effects or to give emphasis when outlining in backstitch.

There is no need to limit yourself solely to stranded cotton (floss). Wonderful effects can be achieved by substituting different threads. You will see that in this book many different threads have been used – flower thread, fine wool, metallics, space-dyed thread, as well as the more usual stranded cotton (floss). Try experimenting: a rather ordinary piece of work can be transformed by substituting or adding a thread you may not have thought of using before.

USING SPACE-DYED OR VARIEGATED THREAD

Wonderful effects can be achieved if these threads are used sympathetically. For example, a simple design (such as 'Assisi birds', page 108) can be transformed by substituting spaced-dyed thread for a single colour.

When using variegated thread (so called because the colour gradually changes from a very pale to a darker shade of the same colour), it is important to select the lengths carefully to ensure that the change of colour is gradual throughout your stitching; that is, avoid placing dark thread directly next to a light one. Beautifully subtle effects can be achieved in your embroidery as the colours gently merge and the shades vary.

On the other hand, some space-dyed threads are dyed with sudden and dramatic changes of colour at quite short intervals, giving a totally different look. For both types of thread, if you are working in cross stitch, it is important to complete each cross individually, not to work a line of half crosses and then complete by working back along the line.

THREAD STORAGE

It makes sense to store your threads in an organized and efficient manner so that you can see and select the colours for your chosen project at a glance. There are many methods of thread storage, ranging from cards with holes punched in them which hold the cut skeins, to storage boxes with cards to wrap threads around. Other sophisticated thread organizers that store threads in plastic pockets, which are then housed in a binder, can also be purchased.

Whichever method you choose (including your own versions of the above), storing your threads carefully will ensure that they are clean, tangle-free and freely available for selection.

NEEDLES

You will need blunt tapestry needles for all types of counted needlework. The most commonly used sizes are 22, 24, 26 and the more recently introduced 28. The higher the number, the finer the needle. The size selected will depend on the fabric used: for example, size 22 for 8-count Aida, size 26 for fine 30- to 32-count linen. The needle should offer a little pressure when passed through the fabric and should not be able to drop right through the hole. Special long, fine needles are available for beading. Always try to keep a large assortment in stock.

HOOPS AND FRAMES

I am often asked whether it's better to work with or without a hoop or frame. This is an impossible question to answer: half of all embroiderers work with a hoop or frame and the other half without. Neither is right nor wrong; it's simply a matter of comfort and convenience. I know there is a school of thought that says more regular stitching will be achieved with a hoop or frame (and I personally go along with this theory), but if you find either a hoop or frame awkward to use, then your stitching will be an unhappy affair and this will show in the finished work.

If you decide to use an embroidery hoop, always use one that is big enough to house the complete design comfortably. This will ensure that the hoop never needs to be placed over any stitching and will not spoil the completed work with pulled and snagged stitches. None of the designs in this book are bigger than 7in (18cm) square, so the range of embroidery hoops currently available will house them nicely. To prevent your fabric slipping about, and also to protect it from the wood, it is advisable to bind both the inner and outer hoops with white bias binding secured with a few stitches.

Another way to protect your work from hoop marks is to place a piece of tissue paper between the fabric and hoop, then tear away the middle section to expose the area to be worked. Hoops tend to leave crease marks that are almost impossible to remove, so remember to remove the hoop *every* time you finish working.

Larger pieces of work will require a rectangular frame. These come in many sizes and are particularly useful when working in tent stitch which tends to distort fabric. First, strengthen the edges of your fabric by hemming or binding with tape. Then, sew the top and bottom edges of the fabric to the webbing which is attached to the rollers of the frame. It is important to ensure that the fabric is placed evenly in the frame – if attached unevenly it will become distorted. Assemble the frame and lace the side edges of the fabric to the stretchers with very strong thread (see Fig 2).

A quicker and easier, though just as effective, way of keeping your fabric taut is to use an interlocking bar frame. These can be purchased individually or in multi-packs which

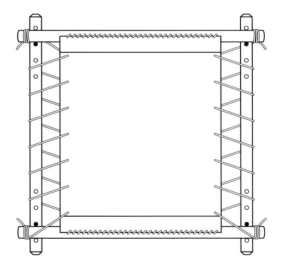

Fig 2 A rectangular embroidery frame.

enable you to make up to twenty-seven different square and rectangular frames. The fabric is stapled straight on to the frame (or attached with drawing pins), thus saving a great deal of time and effort. Although less elegant than roller frames, I feel they have many advantages – there are no protruding corners to catch your thread on, they are extremely light to hold, easier to store and more portable.

ADHESIVES

For some of the projects you will need to use glue; for example, when making a fabric covered mount. There are many adhesives available, but I always prefer to use UHU glue, which is recommended for use with fabric, and dries on impact. Also, the fumes associated with this type of product are less obvious with this particular brand.

STITCH DIRECTORY

Most of the projects in this book are worked with stitches that can be classified as 'counted thread' stitches, mainly cross stitch and tent stitch, the exceptions being French knots and free satin stitch (used in the 'Temple Flowers' project). Most of the designs are on a small scale, and for this reason tent stitch over one thread of fabric has been used extensively throughout the book. Because this is a diagonal stitch, it will distort the fabric and the use of a frame is therefore advised. Take care when working over one thread of fabric not to pull the stitch too tightly, as this will result in the embroidery thread slipping behind the warp threads of the fabric.

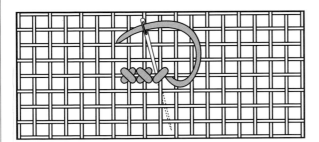

Cross stitch over one thread

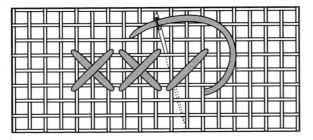

Cross stitch over two threads

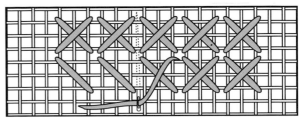

Lines of full cross stitches

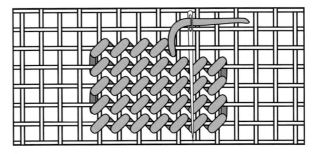

Half cross stitch

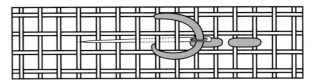

Back stitch

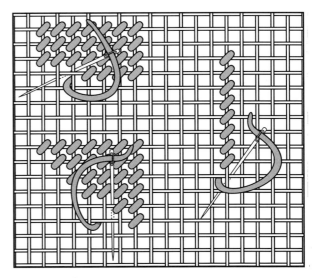

Tent stitch

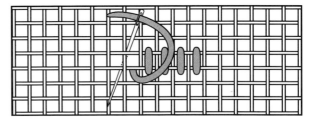

Satin stitch

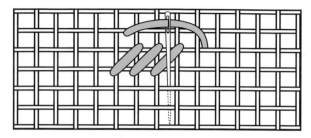

Diagonal satin stitch over two threads

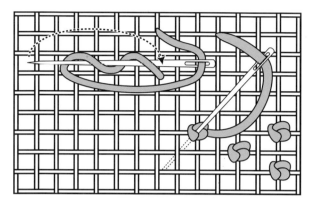

French knot

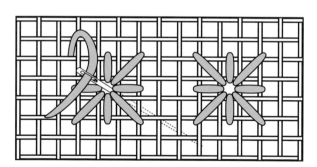

Eyelet stitch/Algerian eye

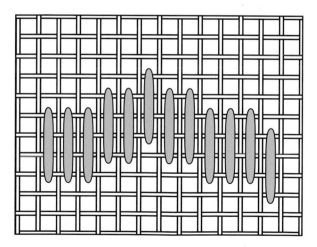

Bargello

BEADWORK

Beadwork is an easy technique to master, and once learned will bring added interest to your work. A beadwork chart looks the same as any type of counted needlework chart, the only difference being that the squares represent beads instead of stitches.

You will need to use a beading needle. This is simply a long, fine needle with a very narrow eye which is able to pass easily through the bead. Match your sewing thread to the colour of your fabric. Polyester sewing thread is a good choice, as it is strong and thin, but if you are stitching lots of beads to your work, it is best to use quilting thread which is even stronger and will hold the beads more securely. If you are only adding a few beads, simply use one strand of the stranded cotton (floss) you are stitching with.

The beads are usually attached with a half cross stitch. However, if you are working on quite a large piece, tent stitch is a better option as it will hold the beads more securely so that they don't sag on the fabric. Bring your needle up through the fabric as you would for half cross stitch. Thread the bead on to the needle (you will probably find it is easier to pick up the bead by 'stabbing' it with the needle itself rather than using your fingers), and insert it into the fabric, completing the stitch. Bring the needle up for the next stitch in the same way and continue.

USING WASTE CANVAS

You can apply a charted design to a fabric without an evenweave by using waste canvas, a specially prepared canvas available in different counts. Simply cut a piece of waste canvas slightly bigger than the overall finished design size and tack (baste) into position on to the right side of the chosen fabric or item of clothing. Find the centre of your charted design and match this to the piece of canvas and fabric. Stitch the design through the canvas and the fabric underneath. When you have completed the stitching, spray the whole design with water (a plant spray is ideal for this purpose); then, using tweezers, remove the soaked threads of the waste canvas one by one. Leave the finished embroidery to dry and press on the wrong side.

The waste canvas method further adds to the versatility of the designs in this book. You could, for example, stitch the 'Bird of Paradise' design, page 94, to the front of a plain sweatshirt, transforming a rather utilitarian garment into a unique fashion statement!

How to make a tassel

1 Cut a piece of stiff card to the length you wish the tassel to be. Wind the thread around the card until the required thickness is achieved. If you are making a set of tassels, keep count of the number of times you wind around the card so that all the tassels will be the same. The type of thread and number of lengths used will depend on the project it is to be used for. For example, silk or rayon thread is ideal for delicate projects, and thick cotton or wool for those of a more robust nature.

2 Thread a needle with a long piece of the same colour thread. Pass it under the wound threads at the top, next to the card (Fig 3a), and tie securely leaving two trailing threads of the same length. Do not fasten off.

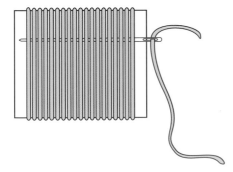

Fig 3a Wind the threads around the card and pass the needle beneath them.

3 Cut the bound threads at the bottom of the card to release them (Fig 3b).

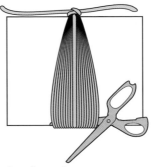

Fig 3b Cut the threads.

4 Thread both of the ends used to tie the tassel into the needle, pass through the top of the tassel and bring out ½in (1.5cm) down, or less for a smaller tassel (Fig 3c).

Fig 3c Tie the tassel.

5 Wind thread tightly several times around the tassel to form the head. Knot securely and pass the needle back through the bound threads to the top (Fig 3d). Use this remaining thread to attach the tassel to the article.

Fig 3d Wind the thread to form the head.

HOW TO MAKE A TWISTED CORD

1 Assess the length of cord you require and then cut a length of thread which is three times as long.

2 Make a loop in each end of the thread and then attach one end to a hook or doorknob (Fig 4a).

Fig 4a Make a loop in each end of the cords.

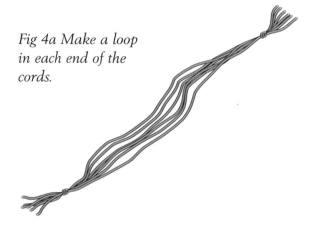

3 Slip a pencil through the other end and, keeping the thread taut, begin twisting the pencil round and round until, when it is released, the thread begins to twist back on itself (Fig 4b).

Fig 4b Twist the cords together.

4 Keeping the threads taut, fold the twisted length in half, matching the ends together (Fig 4c). Stroke along the cord to even out the twists. Finally, tie the ends together. If a thicker cord is required, simply use more strands of thread intially.

Fig 4c Fold the cord in half.

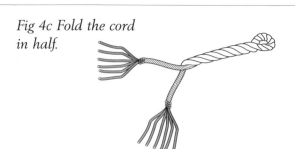

CHARTING NAMES AND DATES

If you wish to add your name or the date to the embroidery, this is a relatively easy process.

Work out your details in pencil on graph paper, adjusting the space to suit the letter chosen. For example, a lower case 'i' placed next to a lower case 'l' usually looks better with two spaces between if the alphabet is very plain, even if only one space is allowed between the other letters. This type of adjustment will sometimes be necessary between other letters, and will quickly become apparent during the charting process.

When you have worked out your details, count the number of squares used vertically and horizontally and position the lettering evenly and centrally in the appropriate place on your fabric. A foolproof way of ensuring accuracy is to photocopy the chart and then mark the position of your details lightly in pencil on the photocopy.

CHARTING YOUR OWN DESIGNS

Making a chart of your own design is surprisingly easy. For example, to substitute your own house for the 'Queen Anne House' shown on page 90:

1 Take a good colour photograph of your home, from the front if you want it to resemble the example shown, although the principle for converting to a chart is the same whatever angle you choose.

2 If necessary, enlarge the design on a photocopier to the size you wish your finished work to be. There are now many shops that offer this facility.

3 Place a sheet of tracing graph paper over the design and secure with masking tape to prevent it from slipping about. This is available in various counts which correspond to the thread count of fabric; so if, for example, you wish to work on 14-count Aida, choose 14-count tracing graph paper. Trace the design on to the graph paper, squaring up the design and eliminating any unnecessary details.

4 Colour in the design using coloured crayons. At this stage, you may want to consider just how life-like you wish your interpretation to be and limit the number of colours you use accordingly. Also, consider blending threads, that is, using two different shades together. This method is particularly effective for roofs. The chart is now ready to stitch from.

HOW TO ENLARGE
AND REDUCE CHARTED DESIGNS

Charted designs are extremely versatile and very easy to enlarge or reduce. As all the designs in this book are small in size and in the main worked on very fine fabrics it is essential to know how to enlarge them. If, for example, you like the look of a particular design but would despair of having to work on fabrics you are unused to, or risk straining your eyes in the process, the following suggestions should help:

∾ Simply change the thread count of the suggested fabric to one you are happy working with. For example, a design with a stitch count of 96 x 96 worked over one thread of Belfast linen with 32 threads per inch, will have a finished size of 3 x 3in (8 x 8cm). The same design worked on Dublin linen with 25 threads per inch (much easier to see) will be 4 x 4in (10 x 10cm). Although this is not a huge increase in size it's worth it if it means you can actually stitch a design that you would otherwise be unable to.

Study the examples on page 9 to see what a difference a change of fabric can make.

∾ If your eyesight is not the problem, but you wish to increase the size of a design to use for another purpose – say a small picture into a cushion, or the 'Miniature Sampler' (page 96) to one of a more usual size – try working the stitches over two, three or even four threads or blocks of fabric. For example, if you work over four threads instead of two, the design will double in size. Likewise, if the instructions state that the design is worked in cross stitch over two threads of linen and you work over just one thread in either cross stitch or tent stitch, the design size will be halved.

∾ Consider every square in the design to be two, three or even four stitches square instead of one. For example, to triple the design size, work a block of stitches three by three for every one stitch shown.

By using any of the methods described here, you will be able to use and enjoy all the charted designs shown regardless of their intricacy. Changing the scale or fabric will also bring greater variety to your work and thus increase the usefulness of any charted design.

HOW TO BEGIN WORKING

FINDING THE CENTRE OF THE FABRIC

Fold your fabric in half and half again and crease lightly. Tack (baste) along these lines in a contrasting sewing thread. The centre of the fabric is where the lines cross. Most instructions suggest that you begin work at this point – this is to ensure that your work is placed centrally, avoiding the horrible possibility of working off the edge of the fabric. My picture framer often tells me horror stories of work presented to her for framing with only two or three threads left at the edge of the stitching.

If, however, you want to start work at, say,

the top left-hand corner of the design (and this often seems to be a more logical alternative with designs that include a border), you must carefully calculate where to start stitching by deducting the design size from your fabric size and positioning accordingly. For example, if your fabric size is 12 x 10in (30.5 x 25.5cm) and your design size 8 x 6in (20.5 x 15cm), you will have 4in (10cm) of spare fabric. You should therefore measure 2in (5cm) down from the top edge and 2in (5cm) in from the side edge and begin work here.

STARTING TO STITCH

The following list should help you to achieve perfection!

∾ Cut your thread into pieces no longer than 12–18in (30.5–45.5cm), and even shorter for metallic thread. Many stitchers make the mistake of thinking that if they thread their needles with long lengths it will save time constantly re-threading needles. Longer lengths, however, tangle more easily (metallic threads in particular) and stitching can take even longer. Long lengths of thread can also become very 'tired' looking at the end of the length and lose their lustrous appearance.

∾ When using stranded cotton (floss) always separate and untwist all six strands before selecting the number of strands required. (The amount will depend on the fabric used.) It really is worth going to this trouble every time, as the threads lie flatter and give greater coverage.

∾ Never use a knot to begin stitching. Knots can pull through the fabric and will give a bumpy finish which will spoil the appearance of your work. To begin stitching previously unworked fabric, bring the needle up through the fabric leaving about 1in (2.5cm) of thread at the back. Holding the thread in place, work three or four stitches

until the trailing thread is caught and secured (Fig 5). To begin a new thread on fabric which has been previously stitched, simply run the needle through the loops of three or four stitches at the back of the work near to where you wish to begin stitching. Bring the needle up at the required place and begin.

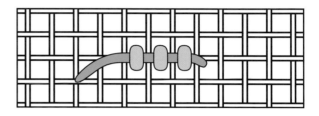

Fig 5 Run a new thread through the back of the existing stitches.

∾ Be careful not to pull stitches too tightly. They should sit evenly on the fabric. Much is always talked about the importance of tension in knitting, but it is just as important in embroidery.

∾ To ensure a smooth even finish to your work, make sure that all top stitches lie in the same direction – it does not matter if this is top left to bottom right or top right to bottom left.

∾ Remember to 'drop' your needle every four or five stitches. This will take the twist out of the thread and avoid tangles.

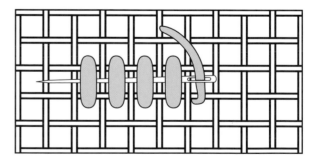

Fig 6 To finish secure the thread on the reverse.

∾ The method for finishing and securing a thread is much the same as starting. Leaving yourself enough thread to finish, take the needle through to the back of the work. Run the needle through the back loop of three or four stitches and snip off the thread close to the stitching (Fig 6).

WORKING THE PROJECT

Embroidery always looks better if it hasn't been washed and ironed, and employing the following simple measures will take care of it, and protect it from getting grubby as you work:

∾ Always wash your hands before beginning to sew.

∾ Store your work in a clean, white pillowcase, or if it's too big, wrap in a clean, white cloth.

∾ Try and dissuade admiring onlookers from running their fingers over the stitches. Beautiful embroidery seems to have a magnetic effect, provoking an almost irresistible urge to touch and run your fingers over the work!

∾ Avoid potential disaster by never drinking tea, coffee or other hazardous liquids near your work.

Skills, such as finishing, mounting and framing a completed piece of embroidery, and making a foldover card, are described at the back of the book (see Finishing Techniques, pages 116–17, and Framing Your Work, pages 118–25). For suppliers of the materials used, see page 126.

Framed initial (see page 25).

THE BOXERS

The idea for this design, with its lines of intricate patterns, came from a 17th–century band sampler. The two figures, now known as 'boxers' because of their pugilistic pose, are believed to originate from a 16th–century Italian pattern depicting lovers exchanging gifts. As so often happens when designs are copied and simplified over the years, their original form has altered, creating a totally different interpretation from what was actually meant to be depicted.

DESIGN SIZE: 3 x 3in (8 x 8cm)
STITCH COUNT: 50 x 52

Cream 32-count Belfast linen, 7 x 7in (18 x 18cm)
DMC stranded cotton (floss) and gold thread as shown in the key

Use one strand of stranded cotton (floss) over two threads of linen. Use the gold thread as it comes – do not separate the strands.

1 Find the centre of the design and work outwards from this point in backstitch and eyelet stitch, following the chart.

2 Stretch, mount and frame as preferred (see Finishing Techniques, page 116 and Framing Your Work, page 118 for further guidance).

OTHER OPTIONS

❧ Try lengthening the design into a mini band sampler by adding tiny backstitch patterns. You will find a multitude to choose from (if you do not wish to design your own) on 17th–century samplers.

❧ Taking into account the original meaning of the 'boxer' figures, use the design for a very special Valentine or wedding card, omitting the border below the figures and inserting the names of the intended couple.

In The Frame

THIS SUBTLY PAINTED FRAME of grey-green and gold with its two arch-shaped mounts came ready-made with a print which I simply removed. I frequently use ready-made frames this way. This is not only a cheaper way of framing your work, but it can also throw up possibilities for framing that you might not have thought of – in this case the arched mounts, which seem to work well. It is often worth buying a particularly nice frame, keeping it until the right project comes along or designing a piece specifically to fit.

If you intend to use an arch-shaped mount as shown, ask your picture framer to cut this for you, as this shape is almost impossible to achieve accurately if cutting freehand.

THE BOXERS

DMC STRANDED COTTON (FLOSS)

— 347 dull red
— D282 gold thread
— 3051 dull green
— 924 antique blue

✳ Eyelet stitch 3051
✺ Eyelet stitch 924
✺ Diamond eyelet stitch 347
☆ Middle point

GOLDEN CHERUB

Cherubs, strangely enough, were originally seen as terrifying
creatures with demonic smiles and many heads who stood at the entrance to
paradise and guarded celestial palaces and kingdoms. They bore
no resemblance to the curly-haired babies they became during the Renaissance
and our accepted idea of them today. This tiny golden cherub is set within an
elaborate corner motif worked in gold thread – exquisite
and simplicity itself to make. Resin, plastic or plaster cherubs are widely
available from gift shops, you may even have one tucked away
with your Christmas decorations.

DESIGN SIZE: Including cherub, 2½ x 2¾ in
   (6 x 7cm)
STITCH COUNT: 49 x 49

Dark green 25-count Dublin linen, 6 x 6in (15 x
   15cm)
DMC gold thread D282
One cherub approximately 2in (5cm) tall
Piece of card, 3 ½ x 3 ½ in (9 x 9cm)
Glue/impact adhesive
Gold frame of your choice to fit the card. If you are
   buying a ready-made frame, simply adjust the size
   of the card and fabric to fit

Use the gold thread as it comes – do not separate
the strands – and work cross stitch over one thread of
fabric.

1 Measure 1¾ in (4.5cm) in from the left
side of your fabric and 1¾ in (4.5cm) up
from the bottom. Position the bottom left
corner stitch of the design at the point these
two measurements cross. Work from this
point following the chart.

2 Stretch the finished embroidery over the
card (see Finishing Techniques, pages
116–17, and Framing Your Work, pages
118–25) and glue the cherub into place as
shown in the photograph. No exact marking
is given on the chart for positioning the
cherub, as yours could be a slightly different
shape or size from the one shown. If you are
very keen to house the design behind glass,
you will need to use a box frame – your picture framer will be able to make one for you.

In The Frame

AS THE DESIGN was worked in gold thread and mounted with a gold cherub, a gold frame was the obvious choice. I chose a simple frame, one that I thought would benefit from an equally simple antique effect known as 'spotting' – flicking small amounts of varnish on to the gold finish with a stiff brush. An unusual alternative would be to work the design in dark grey thread on a subtle beige-pink fabric, and house it in a tiny ornate frame painted dark pink-maroon then overpainted with light grey which is wiped off the raised area to let the darker colour show. through.

OTHER OPTIONS

❧ Replace the cherub with an initial worked in either gold thread or space-dyed thread as shown in the additional project on page 19. Use the alphabet for the 'Tulips and Lavender Initials', page 111.

❧ Substitute a stitched cherub. You will find cherub designs in books containing sampler motifs – see Bibliography, page 127.

❧ Use the design to decorate a tiny golden box lid. See Suppliers, page 126, for boxes.

GOLDEN CHERUB

DMC Metallic thread
▪▪ D282 gold

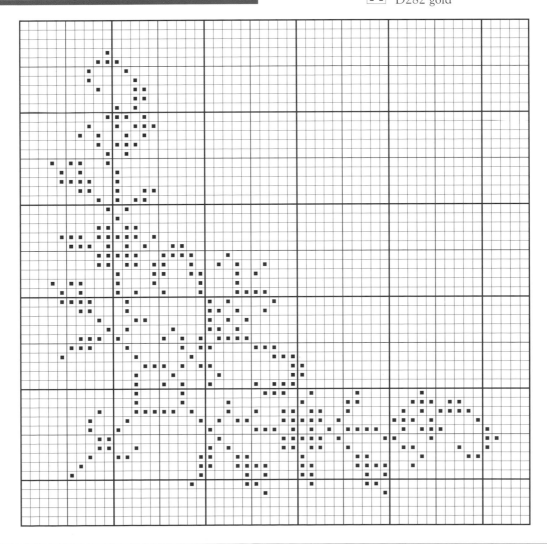

BIRDS AND CHERRIES

Repeating a motif has been popular with artists and embroiderers, throughout history. Elizabethan embroidery with its abundance of acorn, pineapple and tulip borders, the stylized repeat patterns of European peasant embroidery, the lavish embroidery of eastern Mediterranean countries, and the colourful silk embroideries of India, all show that repeat design was a major influence. This particular design – a collection of motifs and patterns – is surrounded with a striped border.

DESIGN SIZE: 3½ x 3½ in (9 x 9cm)
STITCH COUNT: 85 x 87

Yellow 22-count petit point canvas, 7 x 7in (18 x 18cm)
DMC Medici crewel wool (yarn) and stranded cotton (floss) as shown in the key

Work in tent stitch using two strands of crewel wool (yarn), or two strands of stranded cotton (floss) where appropriate, over one thread of canvas. As tent stitch tends to distort the canvas, use a frame to keep your work straight.

In The Frame

AGAIN, I FOUND A READY-MADE FRAME and mount in just the right colours for this design – I think the grey and gold match the embroidery particularly well. If you work the sampler in alternate colourways, try matching the mount to one of the shades you have used. Or, if you are using a double mount, try picking out two of the colours.

1 Find the centre of the design and work outwards from this point in tent stitch, following the chart.

2 When the design is complete, stretch, mount and frame your finished work as preferred (see Finishing Techniques, pages 116–17, and Framing Your Work, pages 118–25 for more advice).

OTHER OPTIONS

∾ I think this particular design would work well as a cushion. If worked in cross stitch over two threads of 10-count interlock canvas with DMC tapestry wool (yarn), the design size will be 17 x 17in (43 x 43cm).

∾ Instead of the subtle shades used here, try a dramatic change of colour, say emerald green, kingfisher blue and gold. This will give the design a completely different look.

∾ Individual elements from the design could easily be used for a border design – the row of storks could be added to a birth sampler for example.

DMC Medici wool (yarn)

- 8107 pink-brown
- 8504 pale beige
- 8201 antique blue-green
- 8931 dark grey-blue
- 8119 pale mauve-pink
- 8123 dark plum

DMC Stranded cotton (floss)

- 413 dark grey
- 3743 very pale lilac
- 819 palest pink
- 3371 very dark brown
- 3778 light apricot
- 926 grey-blue
- 3761 soft pale turquoise
- 775 very pale blue
- 924 dark antique blue
- 915 maroon
- 3607 cerise
- 906 mid sage green
- 950 pale pink-beige
- 3042 mauve
- 340 dark lilac
- 554 mid mauve
- ☆ Middle point

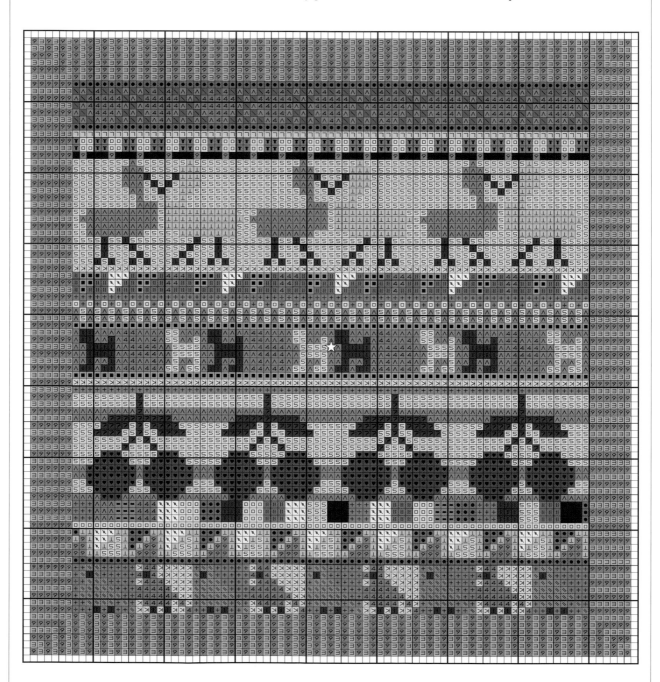

Yellow Birds

The full title of the piece from which this design was taken is 'Landscape With Yellow Birds', painted in 1923 by my favourite artist of the period, Paul Klee. The original with its scrawny yellow birds is one of his most admired works, and can be classified as one of his 'dream' pictures. A fantasy design, Klee includes European fir trees in a tropical jungle setting of both night and day.

DESIGN SIZE: 4 x 4in (10 x 10cm)
STITCH COUNT: 96 x 96

White petit point 22-count canvas, 8 x 8in (20 x 20cm)
DMC stranded cotton (floss) as shown in the key

Work in tent stitch, using two strands of stranded cotton (floss) over one thread of canvas. As tent stitch tends to distort the canvas, use a frame to keep your work straight.

1 Find the centre of the design and work outwards from this point in tent stitch, following the chart.

2 Stretch, mount and frame as preferred (see Finishing Techniques, pages 116–17, and Framing Your Work, pages 118–25 for more advice).

OTHER OPTIONS

❧ Work a small section of the design to create a striking greetings card. Alternatively work an even smaller section for a framed miniature picture.

❧ Don't limit yourself to smaller items, as this design would work just as well in wool on larger mesh canvas for use as either a cushion, rug or wall hanging.

In The Frame

BECAUSE THIS IS A VERY MODERN DESIGN, I decided to use a very simple frame and mounts. The three mounts are grey with a black core, so when the framer cut the aperture with a 45 degree angle, the colour of the inner card showed black instead of white – an extremely dramatic result. Framers usually stock a variety of colours with this option, and it is worth bearing this in mind as a useful and unusual alternative.

YELLOW BIRDS

Right: Yellow Birds (bottom) and Llamas (top).

LLAMAS

Worked in the colours of ancient Andean textiles in traditional Peruvian patterns, the unusual and striking miniature pictured on page 31 has llamas as its central theme. Latin American folk art has traditionally featured wonderfully rich, earthy colours used in a totally unrestrained way. Peruvian ceramics, woven textiles, furniture and clothing, all show similar design influences deep-rooted in ethnic tradition.

DESIGN SIZE: 5½ x 3in (14 x 8cm)
STITCH COUNT: 122 x 67

White 22-count petit point canvas, 8 x 6in
  (20 x 15cm)
DMC Medici crewel wool (yarn) and stranded cotton
  (floss) as shown in the key

Work in tent stitch, using two strands of crewel wool (yarn) or two strands of stranded cotton (floss) over one thread of canvas. As tent stitch tends to distort the canvas, use a frame to keep your work straight.

1 Find the centre of the design and work outwards from this point in tent stitch, following the chart.

2 Stretch, mount and frame as preferred (see Finishing Techniques, pages 116–17, and Framing Your Work, pages 118–25, for more advice).

OTHER OPTIONS

∾ Use either the outer border or the inner panel repeated and extended in length until long enough to make a belt. For the perfect finish, add an antique silver buckle. Antique markets are good places to hunt for this sort of thing, but if you can't find what you want, most haberdashers are able to supply reasonable alternatives.

∾ Work the design on rug canvas in cross stitch, with several lengths of wool in your needle, to make a truly unusual rug or wall hanging.

∾ Use part of the centre panel, worked in stranded cotton to reduce the bulk, as a striking design for a greetings card.

In The Frame

THIS IS ONE of those happy accidental 'try it and see' framing experiences that worked. I originally intended to use a simple black frame (now awaiting a suitable project) but it just didn't work. This ready-made black and walnut frame did, however, so I simply had two pale beige mounts cut to size, and now can't understand why I ever wanted a black frame in the first place!

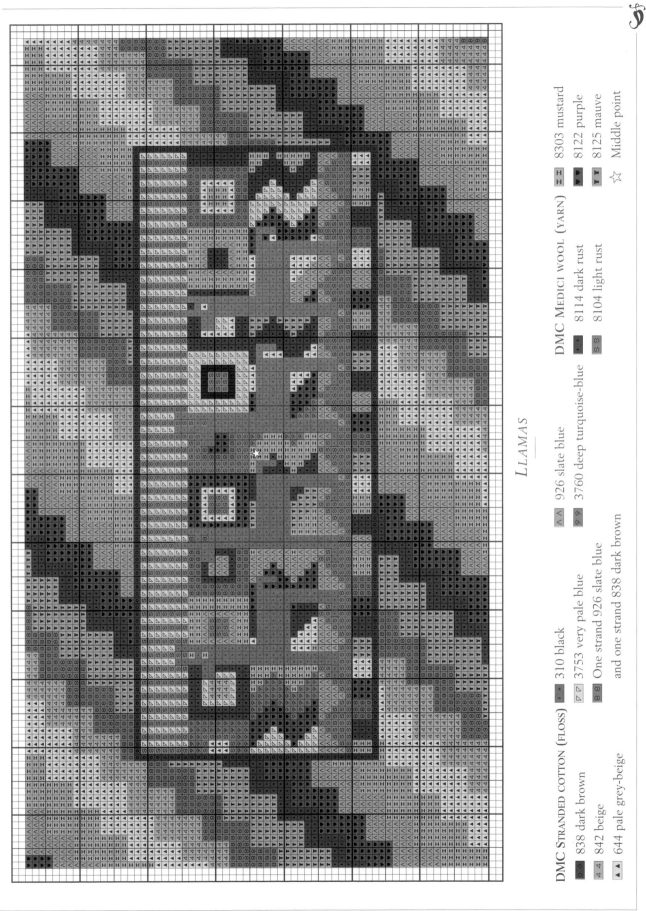

LLAMAS

DMC STRANDED COTTON (FLOSS)

◾	310	black
◪	3753	very pale blue
⊠	838	dark brown
◩	842	beige
◄	644	pale grey-beige

		One strand 926 slate blue
⊞	8 8	and one strand 838 dark brown

⋀	926	slate blue
⧈	3760	deep turquoise-blue

DMC MEDICI WOOL (YARN)

◨	8114	dark rust
⬢	8104	light rust

H	8303	mustard
◣	8122	purple
T	8125	mauve
☆		Middle point

DAMASK MIRROR FRAME

Definitely not meant for checking your hemline, this pretty damask frame
with a tiny mirror is totally impractical, definitely unnecessary,
but thoroughly gorgeous, and the perfect addition to a sumptuous bedroom.
The term 'damask' refers to reversible fabric, originally of silk,
woven with an ornamental and often self-coloured design. Wool damask was
often used in the 18th century for upholstery and curtains
and, due to its classic simplicity, is as popular today as it has ever been.

DESIGN SIZE: 4 ½ x 4 ½ in (11.5 x 11.5cm)
STITCH COUNT: 113 x 113

Dark pink-brown (colour No 432) 25-count Lugana,
   9 x 9in (23 x 23cm)
DMC stranded cotton (floss) as shown in the key
Small mirror, 2 x 2in (5 x 5cm)
Piece of strong card, 4 ½ x 4 ½ in (11.5 x 11.5cm)
Glue/impact adhesive
Piece of backing fabric to match the frame, 5 ½ x 5 ½ in
   (14 x 14cm)
Fine cord (bought or make your own – see page 16)
   in a matching shade, 30in (76cm)
Bought tassel (or make your own – see page 15)
Terylene® wadding, 4 x 4in (10 x 10cm)

Work in tent stitch, using two strands of stranded
cotton (floss) over one thread of fabric. As tent
stitch tends to distort the fabric, use a frame to keep
your work straight.

1 Measure 2 ¼ in (6cm) down from the top
of the fabric and 2 ¼ in (6cm) in from the
side. Begin working the top left-hand corner
of the border design here in tent stitch,
following the chart.

2 Cut a square central aperture in the piece
of card 1 ⅛ x 1 ⅛ in (28 x 28mm).

3 Make up the embroidered fabric as a
mount (see Framing Your Work, page 118).

4 Glue the mirror into place at the back of
the aperture.

5 Lightly glue the wadding on to the back
of the covered mount.

6 Make turnings of approximately ¼ in
(6mm) around the edge of the backing fabric
and stitch to the edge of the covered mount
with tiny invisible stitches so that the
wadding is sandwiched in the middle.

7 Sew the cord to the edge of the frame
where the backing and embroidered fabric
meet, using small invisible stitches. Make a
hanging loop at the top in the middle.

In The Frame

I N THIS CASE, the framing of the piece *is* the piece. Change the fabric or the thread and you create a totally different frame with a totally different feel. For instance, work the whole design in rich gold thread on a dark background. Edge with gold braid, finish with a gold tassel, and you have a really sumptuous mirror frame.

You could, however, add a separate frame and simply use the design as a mount. If you do, paint your frame to match one of the colours. For trying out colours use those tiny pots of paint you can get from DIY shops.

DAMASK MIRROR FRAME

DMC STRANDED COTTON (FLOSS)

⊠ ⊠ 950 very pale pink

■ ■ 407 pink-beige

☆ Middle point

8 With great care, apply a small amount of glue to the edge of the aperture. Do not apply straight from the tube – this is far too risky to even contemplate – but squeeze a little from the tube on to a spare piece of card and apply very carefully with a pin. Starting at a corner, apply the cord to the glued edge, pushing the ends just under the mount so that they do not show.

9 Finally, stitch the tassel securely to the bottom middle of the frame.

OTHER OPTIONS

∽ Use the frame for a photograph instead of a mirror.

∽ Use an alternative colourway to match your decor – blue or green for example.

∽ Use the design with an initial (this option avoids cutting the fabric at all!).

∽ To ensure that this little treasure becomes a family heirloom, work part (or all) of the design in tiny beads.

BEADWORK TULIP

Beadwork was hugely popular in the 19th century and used, in conjunction with Berlin woolwork, for fire screens, footstools, cushions, tea cosies and clothing. There was almost nothing that could not be beaded. If you are new to beading but keen to learn this fascinating technique, this project should appeal. Worked entirely in beads and framed with a sumptuously rich mount (made by covering card with silk), this jewel-like treasure is simplicity itself to make.

DESIGN SIZE: 2 x 2 ¼ in (5 x 6cm)
STITCH COUNT: 33 x 36

Cream 32-count Belfast linen, 5 x 5in (13 x 13cm)
Mill Hill beads as shown in the key
Beading needle
Cream polyester sewing thread

Beading instructions can be found in Workbox on
page 14. Use sewing cotton over two threads of linen.

1 Find the centre of the design and work
outwards from this point, following the
chart.

2 Stretch, mount and frame as preferred
(see Finishing Techniques, pages 116–17,
and Framing Your Work, pages 118–25 for
more advice). If you wish to use a fabric-
covered mount like the one shown for this
design, see page 119.

OTHER OPTIONS

⌁ Work any of the smaller motifs in the
book substituting beads for thread.

⌁ Adding beads to any of the designs shown
will bring a three-dimensional look to your

BEADWORK TULIP

MILL HILL BEADS

■ ■	02011 gold	S S	42018 pale pink
+ +	40374 dark purple-blue	△ △	02020 dark green
◇ ◇	42029 turquoise	● ●	42012 plum
■ ▮	02012 dark plum	☆	Middle point

work. You can substitute the beads in this
design with matching shades of Marlitt
thread, which has a wonderfully shiny finish
and will produce a similar jewel-like result.

In The Frame

I chose a simple frame with a rich gold finish to enhance the shine
of the beads. What makes this piece different, however, is the
fabric-covered mount – dyed silk in fuchsia and orange which boldly
complements the colour of the beads. I'm fond of fabric-covered
mounts as they offer endless possibilities for adding both colour and
texture to almost any project. If you see a particularly nice fabric,
buy a small amount to hoard away. Take the idea one step further
and add sequins, beads, ribbon, lace, buttons – all manner of things
that will add a touch of originality.

TEMPLE OF FLOWERS

India has a rich tradition of embroidery, with wide and varied styles from its many regions. The idea for this design was taken from an exquisitely worked table cover which originated in northern or north-western India. Made in the 1880s it was so ornate and finely executed it must have been the work of a professional embroiderer. The original embroidery on which this design was based was worked in chain stitch and stem stitch, techniques begun and much favoured by the court workshops at Jaipur, Rajasthan, in the 18th century.

DESIGN SIZE: 4½ x 5in (11.5 x 13cm)
STITCH COUNT: 108 x 123

Yellow 22-count petit point canvas, 8 x 9in (20 x 23cm)
DMC metallic thread and stranded cotton (floss) as shown in the key

Use three strands of stranded cotton (floss) over one thread of canvas except for the additional flowers – see specific instructions below. Use the gold thread as it comes – do not separate the strands. As the main body of the design is in tent stitch, which tends to distort canvas, use a frame to keep your work straight.

1 Find the centre of the design and work outwards from this point in tent stitch, following the chart, and working the main body of the design first. Work the background in tent stitch in 890 dark green.

2 Using four strands of dull red stranded cotton (floss) in 347, work the large flowers surrounding the seated figure in long straight stitches. Work several French knots at the centre of the flowers in gold thread.

3 Work smaller flowers (without French knot centres) using two strands of 270 metallic red all over the green background. These flowers are not marked on the chart as it is easier to fill in where necessary.

4 The striped border is worked in diagonal satin stitch over three threads of canvas. Work using three strands of 890 dark green, then oversew with alternate satin stitches in D282 gold and 270 metallic red. Place as shown on the chart.

5 Stretch, mount and frame as preferred (see Finishing Techniques, pages 116–17, and Framing Your Work, pages 118–25).

OTHER OPTIONS

∾ Isolate the central kneeling figure and work it on its own with a plain background. Frame as a miniature with toning mounts of red and green in a tiny gold frame.

∾ Use the design as a centre panel for an ornate cushion. As a finishing touch, add gold braid and brightly coloured tassels.

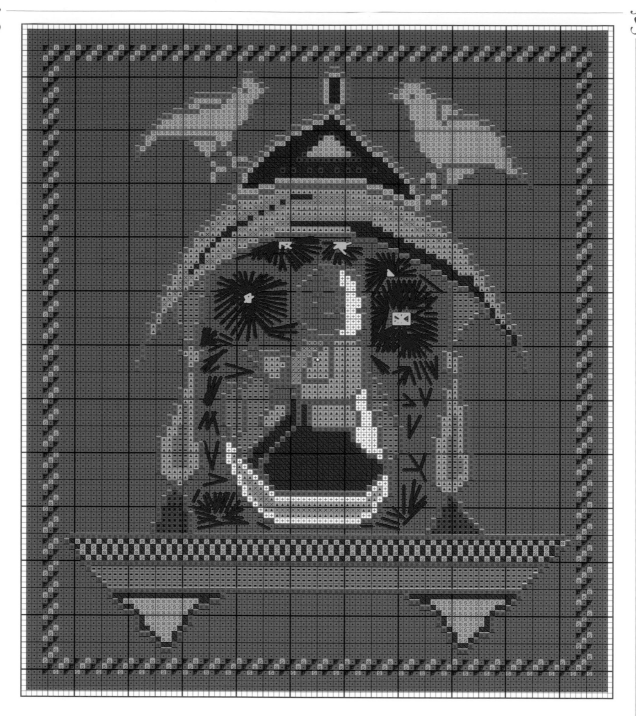

TEMPLE OF FLOWERS

DMC STRANDED COTTON (FLOSS)

+ +	Blanc
I I	3830 dark flesh
✱ ✱	350 pink-red
	666 bright red
✕ ✕	722 mid orange
▲ ▲	3825 light orange
▬ ▬	3051 mid green

• •	890 dark green
▪ ▪	310 black
▬	347 dull red – large satin stitch flowers

DMC METALLIC THREAD

S S	D282 gold
▬	270 red – background flowers
☆	Middle point

In The Frame

I HAD ORIGINALLY intended to use a fabric-covered mount with added sequins for this project and I did actually make one to fit. It looked disastrous! Because the design itself is so complex and busy, the colours and textures fought with and swamped it, proving the maxim 'less is more'. The lesson to be learned, I'm sure, is that the more complex the design, the plainer the mount should be. A simple but brightly coloured motif, however, would look wonderful with an elaborate mount.

REINDEER

Repeating a deer motif on a patterned background, and adding a rather
gnarled tree, makes this a highly unusual piece. The
technique used to create the raised effect for the tree is an easy one to
master: just follow the instructions below. It adds
interest and individuality to the embroidery, and is an idea that could be
successfully used to transform a relatively ordinary piece of work.

DESIGN SIZE: 4¾ x 5¾ in (12 x 14.5cm)
STITCH COUNT: 107 x 130

Yellow 22-count petit point canvas, 8 x 9in (20 x
    23cm)
DMC Medici crewel wool (yarn) and stranded cotton
    (floss) as shown in the key

Use two strands of crewel wool (yarn), or two strands
of stranded cotton (floss) where appropriate, over one
thread of canvas. Refer to key for exceptions. As much
of the design is worked in tent stitch, which tends to
distort canvas, use a frame to keep your work straight.

1 Work all the background first. Find the
centre of the design and work outwards
from this point in tent stitch and horizontal
satin stitch (see key), following the chart.

2 Work the tree in long stitches with DMC
828 stranded cotton (floss), using all six
strands and following the placement on the
chart. Don't worry about positioning the
branches and roots exactly as shown; aim to
create your own version of a gnarled tree.
When you have the 'skeleton' in place,
thread your needle with three strands of the
same thread. Bring the needle up at the base
of any of the branches, and coil the thread

around the long length by oversewing (without taking the needle through the fabric).
When the length is completely covered, take
the needle back through the fabric at the top
of the length and bring it up at the base of
the next 'branch'.

3 Complete all the other branches, the
trunk and the roots in the same way. To

In The Frame

THIS DESIGN definitely called for simple
mounts in muted forest colours, and a
woody frame. Often, the title of a piece will
suggest the type of frame to use – I cannot see
reindeer galloping through elaborately
decorated silver! Because the gnarled roots of
the tree are raised, this design has been
framed without glass. If you would like 'dust-
free' heirlooms, ask your picture framer to
make a box frame. This is simply a frame with
deeper sides, and is particularly successful
housing padded, covered mounts and beads,
sequins and so forth.

achieve a gnarled effect for the roots, work lots of wrapped lengths, overlaying them until you are satisfied with the effect.

4 Stretch, mount and frame as preferred (see Finishing Techniques, pages 116–17, and Framing Your Work, pages 118–25 for more advice).

OTHER OPTIONS

∾ Use the 'wrapping' effect to add interest to any suitable motif – you could work a whole forest in this way.

∾ Use the patterned background (the one shown or your own version) to add interest to a plain motif or initial.

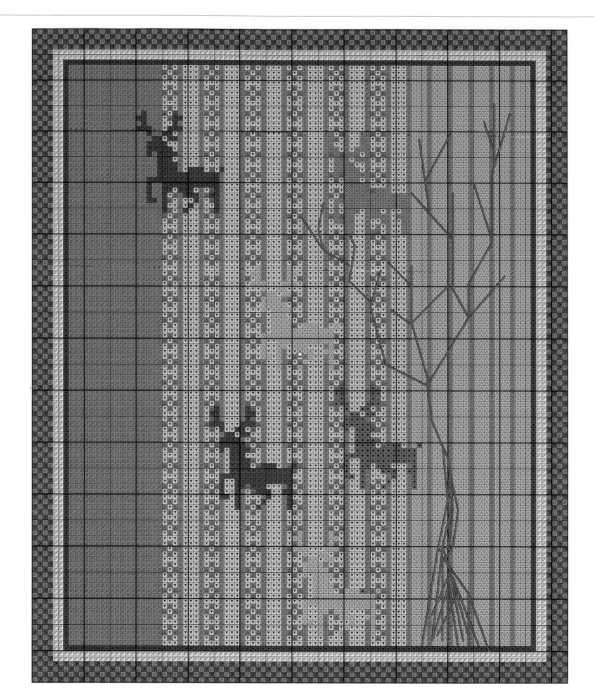

REINDEER

DMC Medici wool (yarn)

- 8120 beige
- 8206 dark blue
- 8207 mid blue
- 8931 grey-blue – tent stitch for reindeer and horizontal satin stitch over three threads for background
- 8504 light beige – horizontal satin stitch over three threads for background stripes, or tent stitch elsewhere

DMC Stranded cotton (floss)

- 3752 pale blue
- 632 warm brown
- 501 grey-green
- 3772 light warm brown
- 828 dark brown – tree
- ☆ Middle point

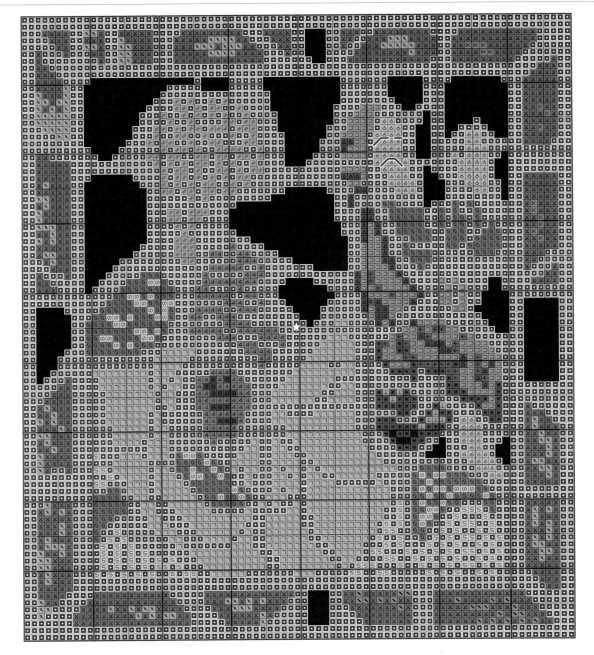

JONAH AND THE WHALE

DMC STRANDED COTTON (FLOSS)

- ■■ 310 black
- ⊓⊓ Two strands 762 very pale grey and one strand 310 black
- 55 743 bright yellow
- ✕✕ 824 dark blue
- ✕✕ Two strands 824 dark blue and one strand 762 very pale grey
- ✕✕ Two strands 762 very pale grey and one strand 824 dark blue

- ╲╲ Two strands 926 mid blue-grey and one strand 762 very pale grey
- ■ 817 rich red
- ⊐⊐ 224 light mauve-pink
- ←← Two strands 224 light mauve-pink and one strand 310 black
- ■ 3801 light bright red
- ⊞⊞ Two strands 722 light orange and one strand 310 black
- 44 722 light orange
- ⁄⁄ 368 soft green

- ⑤⑤ 369 light soft green
- ◎◎ 909 emerald green
- 66 3774 flesh
- ■ Two strands 917 mid-purple and one strand 310 black
- ⊥⊥ 3608 light mauve
- ✳✳ 917 mid purple
- △△ 223 dark mauve-pink
- — Backstitch – one strand 310 black
- ☆ Middle point

JONAH AND THE WHALE

The rich, vibrant colours of this tiny panel show Jonah being ejected from the body of the whale. The design, which dates from about 1280, is part of a remarkable stained-glass window in Cologne Cathedral. The artists of this period were beginning to break away from the stifling practise of always depicting life precisely as it appeared, and felt confident enough to use abstract shapes and strong colours to convey their message. The bright gold, luminous blues, glowing red and deep greens of this stained-glass panel show that these masters of their art put their independence of nature to good use.

DESIGN SIZE: 3¼ x 3½ in (8 x 9cm)
STITCH COUNT: 79 x 90

White 25-count evenweave fabric, 7 x 7in (18 x 18 cm)
DMC stranded cotton (floss) as shown in the key

In The Frame

CARD MOUNTS in colours to match the embroidery plus a gold frame do justice, I think, to this complex design. I purposely used a large frame and large area of mount to surround a relatively small piece, as this is an effective way of drawing the eye into the design. If it had been simply fitted into an ordinary frame, the impact of the strong colours would have been lost. Museums and art galleries often use this method to house small pieces of work in large frames.

Work in tent stitch, using three strands of stranded cotton (floss) over one thread of fabric. As tent stitch tends to distort the fabric, use a frame to keep your work straight.

1 Find the centre of the design and work outwards from this point in tent stitch, following the chart on page 45.

2 Stretch, mount and frame as preferred (see Finishing Techniques, pages 116–17, and Framing Your Work, pages 118–25).

OTHER OPTIONS

∾ Use as the centre panel for a cushion.

∾ Work this design in cross stitch on a larger mesh canvas; make up as a church kneeler.

Right: Jonah and the Whale (top) and Medieval Flowers Bookmark (bottom).

Medieval Flowers Bookmark

The design for this bookmark, pictured on page 47, was based on a stained-glass window from the Middle Ages. The rich jewel-like colours are typical of this period of history and the subject matter, flowers, seem to have been used to decorate almost everything: manuscripts, books, bed hangings, cushions and clothing – all were enhanced with an exuberance of ornamentation. Stained glass can prove to be a stunningly rich source of design for the embroiderer, the vibrant colours and strong shapes translating wonderfully well into fabric and thread.

DESIGN SIZE: 2¾ x 8in (7 x 20cm)
STITCH COUNT: 64 x 189

White 22-count petit point canvas, 6 x 11in (15 x 28cm)
DMC stranded cotton (floss) as shown in the key
Black cotton fabric for backing, 3¼ x 9in (8 x 23cm)
Black sewing thread
Bought tassel (or make your own – see page 15)

Work in tent stitch, using two strands of stranded cotton (floss) over one thread of canvas. As tent stitch tends to distort the canvas, use a frame to keep your work straight.

1 Find the centre of the design and then work outwards from this point in tent stitch, following the chart opposite. To the areas worked in ecru add one or two stitches with one strand of black 310 to give a slightly speckled effect (see the photograph on page 47 for guidance).

2 Stretch the canvas (see Finishing Techniques, pages 116–17 for more advice), then trim to within ¼in (7mm) of the embroidery.

3 Cut the black cotton backing fabric to the same size as the trimmed embroidery and place right sides together. Pin, tack (baste) and either machine or hand stitch together as close to the embroidery as possible; leave the top edge open for turning. Oversew or zig-zag all of the seam edges to strengthen them.

4 Turn the bookmark right sides out and close the opening using small invisible hand stitches.

5 Finally, add either a bought tassel or one you have made yourself from the same coloured threads used in the design, and attach securely to the 'point' at the bottom of the bookmark.

OTHER OPTIONS

∾ Double the size of the design by working in cross stitch over two threads of canvas and make up as a bell pull. Finish in the same way as the bookmark.

∾ Work a small section of the design – just the flower and surrounding area for example – and frame as a miniature.

∾ Enlarge the pattern by repeating both vertically and horizontally and make up into a cushion.

In The Frame

As an alternative to using this design as a bookmark, finish working the embroidery at the base of the second flower so that the design is rectangular, and surround with two card, or fabric-covered, mounts that tone with the colours.

Display in a gold frame – the design would sit happily in one that is elaborately and quite intricately carved.

MEDIEVAL FLOWERS BOOKMARK

DMC Stranded cotton (floss)

+ +	Ecru
s s	676 gold
x x	Two strands 792 blue and one strand 310 black
▪ ▪	310 black
▪ ▪	817 rich red
v v	699 emerald green
☆	Middle point

MYTHICAL BIRD

Majestic and imposing, this mythical creature with its outspread wings is the
centrepiece for an intricate border. Worked in black and
gold thread, this classically styled piece transforms a simple box into a thing
of beauty to be treasured. It is comforting to imagine that
intricate work of this kind, involving many hours of dedicated
stitching may become a prized artifact of future generations.
For this alone, I feel sure it is worth the effort.

DESIGN SIZE: 6¼ x 6¼in (16 x 16cm)
STITCH COUNT: 142 x 142

Yellow 22-count petit point canvas, 10 x 10in
   (25 x 25cm)
DMC stranded cotton (floss) black 310
   and gold thread D282
Purpose-made wooden box with a lid to take an
   embroidery, 6¼ x 6¼in (16 x 16cm), see Suppliers,
   page 126

Work in tent stitch, using two strands of stranded
cotton (floss) over one thread of canvas. Use the gold
thread as it comes – do not separate the strands. As
tent stitch tends to distort the canvas, use a frame to
keep your work straight.

1 Find the centre of the design and work
outwards from this point in tent stitch, following the chart. Work four rows in D282
gold thread surrounding the border.

2 Stretch the canvas (see Finishing
Techniques, pages 116–17, for more advice),
then fit the embroidery into the box lid
carefully following the manufacturer's
instructions.

OTHER OPTIONS

꒰ This design would make a wonderful
church kneeler. Double the design size by
working in cross stitch over two threads of
canvas.

꒰ Frame as a picture, adding several black
and gold mounts, and house in a gold frame.

꒰ Use part of the border with an added gold
tassel (see page 15) to make a very special
bookmark (for a family bible for example).

In The Frame

A WONDERFUL ALTERNATIVE to housing this
design on a box lid would be to frame it
with a number of gold and black mounts in a
black frame. Ask at your picture framers to see
if they supply 'corners'. These are little addi-
tions, usually made of brass, that you can add
to plain frames. In this case, they would look
particularly effective on a plain black frame.

MYTHICAL BIRD

DMC STRANDED COTTON (FLOSS)

- ■■ 310 black
- ·· D282 gold thread

Work four rows in gold thread surrounding the border.

☆ Middle point

EXQUISITE COUNTRY

I chose the title 'Exquisite Country' because I think it shows that even a simple piece can be exquisite in its simplicity. The subject – tiny houses repeated in a 'quilt block' style – has been worked in a wonderful space-dyed thread which adds interest and verve. The twig frame is an unusual idea that adds further interest, but a simple wooden frame would suit the piece equally well.

DESIGN SIZE: 3½ x 3¼ in (9 x 8cm)
STITCH COUNT: 46 x 40

6 x 6in (15 x 15cm) 25-count Lugana colour No 906
DMC stranded cotton (floss) dark navy 939 and CARON Watercolours cranberry 070

Use three strands of stranded cotton (floss), or one of Watercolour thread, over two threads of fabric.

EXQUISITE COUNTRY

××	DMC 939 dark navy
■■	CARON Watercolours cranberry 070
☆	Middle point

Chart for single house design.

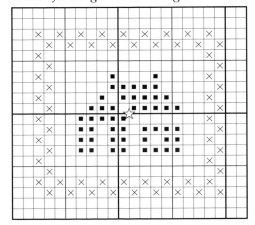

1 Find the centre of the design and work outwards from this point in cross stitch, following the chart below. Remember to work each cross stitch individually; do not work a line of half crosses and then complete it by working back along the line (see Using Space-dyed or Variegated Thread, page 11).

2 Stretch, mount and frame as preferred (see Finishing Techniques pages 116–17, and Framing Your Work, pages 118–25).

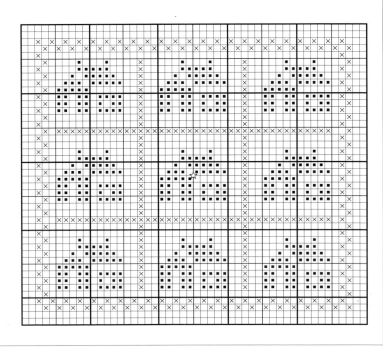

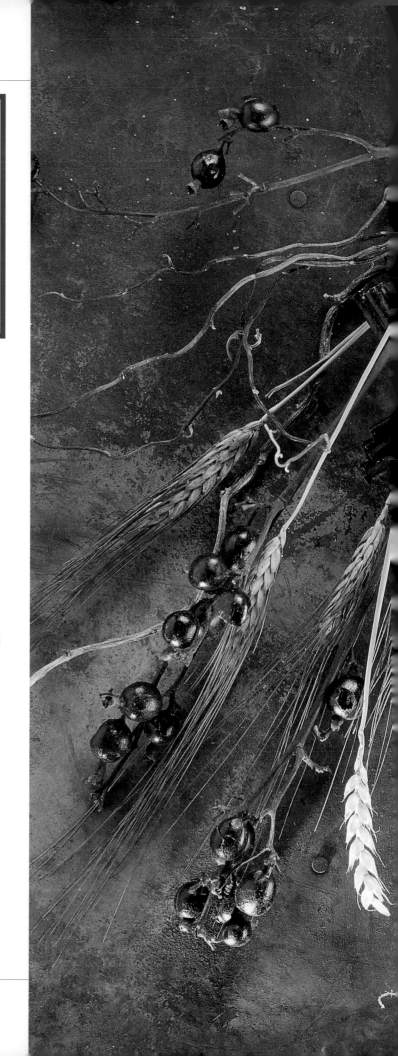

In The Frame

THIS RUSTIC FRAME was made by gluing twigs to a flat wooden frame, overlapping the corners and tying them together. Try working the design in paler colours – seaside shades of pale blue, cream, light orange, etc – and use driftwood instead of twigs to frame the finished piece.

OTHER OPTIONS

∾ Use the design for a greetings card.

∾ Make up the design as a pin cushion.

∾ Use as the centre panel for a cushion. Log cabin patchwork in toning colours would work particularly well for the surround. Exquisite country at its best!

∾ Use the design to decorate the pocket of a pair of child's dungarees (for Using Waste Canvas, see pages 14–15).

∾ Work a line of the houses on a child's bed sheet and pillowcase in a single colour. Use waste canvas as above. As the motif for this design is such a simple shape, you could make up a stencil and follow through with the house theme on any painted finish in the room.

∾ Work a single house using the chart on page 53, and surround with the border and frame. The small frame in the photograph is made from tiny ice-lolly sticks glued at the corners and stained navy.

The larger Exquisite Country picture in its rustic frame is shown here next to the single house design.

WAITING BIRDS

Why waiting birds? Well, whether in a group or alone, as in these two designs, they look so still and patient, as if they're waiting for just the right worm to wriggle its way up to the surface! I love birds, and spend a ridiculous amount of time gazing out of my kitchen window, watching them when I should be writing. This project is really an appeasement of my guilty conscience – all that time spent gazing was positive research.

DESIGN SIZE: 4 x 5¼in (10 x 13.5cm)
STITCH COUNT: 65 x 85

Beige 14-count single thread canvas, 8 x 10in (20 x 25cm)
DMC Medici crewel wool (yarn) and stranded cotton (floss) as shown in the key

Use two strands of crewel wool (yarn), or three strands of stranded cotton (floss) where appropriate, over one thread of canvas. As most of the design is worked in tent stitch, which tends to distort canvas, use a frame to keep your work straight.

In The Frame

THE LARGER and smaller versions of this design are both framed in the same way, using toning card mounts and gold frames. I did try using a slightly spotty fabric-covered mount for the larger version, but it looked far too busy and unnecessary. It is true to say that in the majority of cases a plain mount is most suitable for all but the plainest of pieces.

1 Find the centre of the design and work outwards from this point in tent stitch (apart from the centre panels of the large birds, which should be worked in vertical satin stitch), following the chart.

2 Stretch, mount and frame as preferred (see Finishing Techniques, pages 116–17, and Framing Your Work, pages 118–25).

OTHER OPTIONS

 I think this design would look stunning if used for a cushion. To increase the size, use a larger mesh canvas – say 10-count – and work in cross stitch over two threads.

 To make a square, add another couple of lines of border at the sides of the design.

 Work a line of the large birds with the background shown, and make up into a belt.

 Use part of the centre panel design (extending the length as necessary) and make up as a spectacles case.

Right: Waiting Birds (bottom) and a single bird (top).

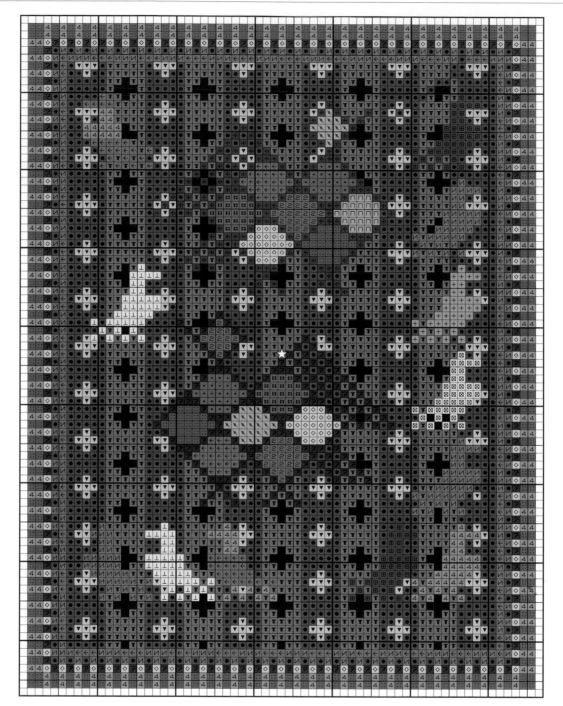

Waiting Birds (group)

DMC Medici wool (yarn)

- 8120 light pink-beige
- 8205 very dark blue
- 8931 mid blue
- 8799 light blue
- 8136 dark maroon
- 8300 chocolate brown
- 8223 rose-pink
- 8175 orange-brown
- 8841 mid beige
- 8397 pale lilac
- 8122 plum pink
- 8108 dark pink-beige
- 8125 pink-beige
- ☆ Middle point

DMC Stranded cotton (floss)

- 977 rich gold-brown
- 926 grey-blue
- 760 warm pink
- 819 palest pink
- 920 dark rust
- 739 very light gold-brown
- 738 light gold-brown

This large imposing bird, charted below, was originally from a Guatamalan design and has been adapted for this embroidery. It is so distinctive that I thought it worth the effort to work on its own. This is an idea you might like to try with any other suitable embroidery – simply isolate a motif and surround it with suitable patterns and borders, then frame it as an unusual miniature.

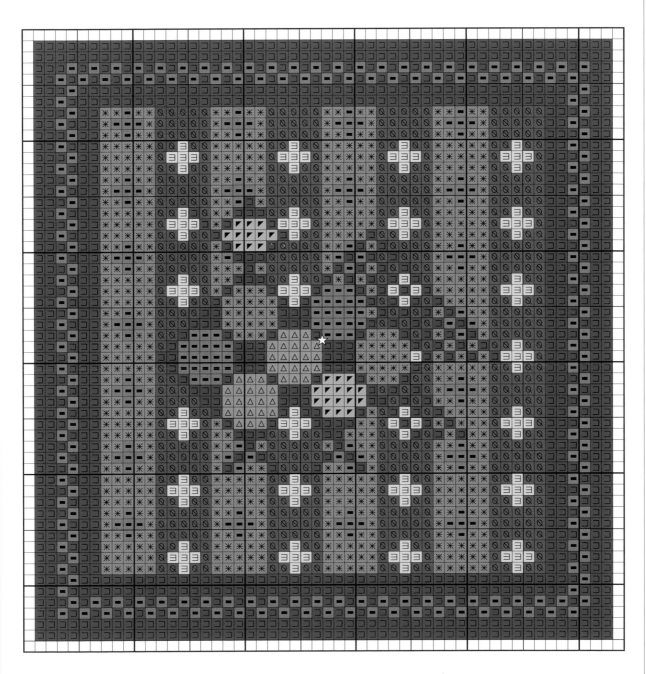

WAITING BIRDS (SINGLE)

DMC STRANDED COTTON (FLOSS)

347 dull red	3731 pink-brown	895 very dark green
3712 apricot	563 light green	732 mid sage green
	3348 apple green	☆ Middle point

FLOWER POT

Not a traditional choice of subject for a silhouette, but the oversized flower pot shown on page 62 has such a strong sense of balance and symmetry that it works extremely well, showing the intricate shapes to their best advantage.

DESIGN SIZE: 3 x 3in (8 x 8cm)
STITCH COUNT: 95 x 92

White 32-count Belfast linen, 7 x 7in (18 x 18cm)
DMC stranded cotton (floss) black 310

Work in cross stitch, using one strand of stranded cotton (floss) over one thread of linen.

1 Find the centre of the design and work outwards from this point in cross stitch, following the chart.

2 Stretch, mount and frame as preferred (see Finishing Techniques, pages 116–17, and Framing Your Work, pages 118–25).

OTHER OPTIONS

∾ Work the design as shown and make up as a pin cushion edged with a fine black cord.

∾ Use the design for a greetings card.

∾ Use the design as a centre panel for a cushion. Work it as given or work in cross stitch over two threads on a coarser linen – for example, 25-count Dublin will more than double the size.

∾ For a completely different look, substitute space-dyed thread.

∾ Add a border, your initials and the date to transform the design into a sampler.

Silhouettes

THE UNUSUAL ART of making silhouettes – portraits depicting the sitter in black against a white or tinted background – was at its height at the end of the 18th and the beginning of the 19th centuries. Originally called 'shades' or 'profiles', they were later named after the Comptroller General of Louis xv, Etienne de Silhouette.

True silhouettes are known as scissor-cuts, indicating the simplest and probably the earliest method by which they were produced. Many silhouettists of the day cut profiles from black paper, working freehand, and mounted the cut profile on white card. Others preferred to draw the profile first and then cut it out.

The invention of photography in 1826 brought a new competitor on to the scene. Initially, photographs were still quite primitive, but as the technique became more sophisticated and more affordable, silhouettes lost out to their more technological rival.

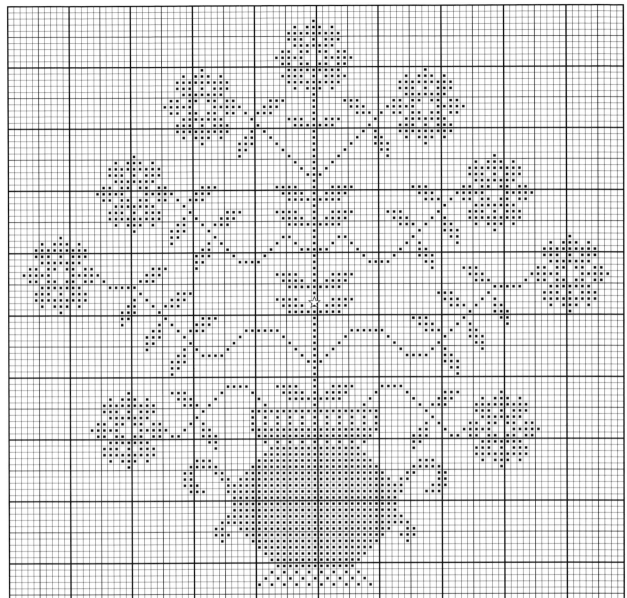

FLOWER POT

**DMC STRANDED COTTON
(FLOSS)**
- ■ ■ 310 black
- ☆ Middle point

In The Frame

BLACK AND GOLD seemed the obvious choice for this project. I chose quite a chunky gold frame, and I think it successfully balances the design. The black mount looked a little too flat and plain, so I rubbed a little black shoe polish into the surface. Finally, I drew a line a little way from the edge of the aperture of the mount (first in pencil with a ruler, then with a gold marker, freehand), and filled the area with Liberon gilt cream (colour Versailles).

VICTORIAN SILHOUETTE

A profile of a Victorian lady is probably the most recognizable form of silhouette. Photography was still in its infancy, and although the heyday of silhouette making had come to an end, many early Victorians still favoured having their profile captured in this way.

DESIGN SIZE: 2 x 3½ in (5 x 9cm)
STITCH COUNT: 62 x 105

White 32-count Belfast linen, 6 x 8in (15 x 20cm)
DMC stranded cotton (floss) black 310

Work in tent stitch, using two strands of stranded cotton (floss) over one thread of linen. As tent stitch tends to distort the fabric, use a frame to keep your work straight.

In The Frame

I LOVE THE MOULDING from which this frame is made – classic simplicity with a Victorian feel. With simple frames of this kind, try the decorator's trick of adding an ornate hanging hook in gilt or brass, or a velvet bow. As these were favourites of the Victorians, they would add to the effect.

Left: A collection of delicate silhouettes. Clockwise from the top these are: Flower Pot (see page 60 for instructions), Tending the Plants (see page 65 for instructions) and Victorian Silhouette.

1 Find the centre of the design and work outwards from this point in tent stitch, following the chart.

2 Stretch, mount and frame as preferred (see Finishing Techniques, pages 116–17, and Framing Your Work, pages 118–25, for more advice).

MAKING A SILHOUETTE

∿ If you would like to chart your own silhouette of a friend or loved one, this is a relatively simple exercise.

Take a photograph of the subject, side on, and enlarge or reduce the image to the size required with the aid of a photocopier – many shops offer this facility.

Place a sheet of tracing graph paper over the image. This is available in various thread counts, so if, for example, you wish to work on 18-count Ainring, choose 18-count tracing graph paper.

Trace the design on to the graph paper, squaring up the design and eliminating any unwanted details. The chart is now ready to stitch from.

For a traditional look, work in black on white fabric, as shown in the example on the opposite page.

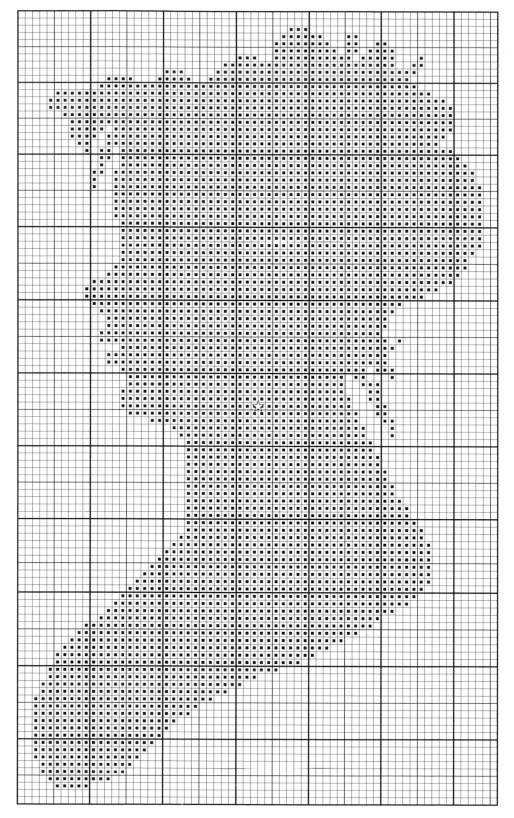

VICTORIAN SILHOUETTE

DMC STRANDED COTTON (FLOSS)

■ ■ 310 black   ☆ Middle point

TENDING THE PLANTS

This design is taken from Torond's silhouette of the Parminter family. The original shows several figures enjoying various activities – reading, playing the piano, netting and, as in the design shown on page 62, watering the plants.

DESIGN SIZE: 1¾ x 2in (4.5 x 5cm)
STITCH COUNT: 59 x 71

Cream 32-count Belfast linen, 5 x 5in (12.5 x 12.5cm)
DMC stranded cotton (floss) black 310

Work in tent stitch, using one strand of cotton (floss) over one thread of linen. As tent stitch tends to distort canvas, use a frame to keep your work straight.

1 Find the centre of the design and work outwards from this point in tent stitch, following the chart.

TENDING THE PLANTS

DMC STRANDED COTTON (FLOSS)
- ■■ 310 black
- ☆ Middle point

2 Stretch, mount and frame as preferred (see Finishing Techniques, pages 116–17, and Framing Your Work, pages 118–25, for more advice).

OTHER OPTIONS

∾ Use the design to decorate the lid of an elegant black trinket pot or the top of a small box.

∾ Make up the design as a greetings card. It could be the ideal thing for a gardening friend perhaps?

In The Frame

THE TINY FRAME for this silhouette originally was all gold. I felt it needed extra impact, so I painted the frame with black eggshell, then applied gilt cream lightly with a soft cloth to the corners and the inner edge beading. The result is much more dramatic.

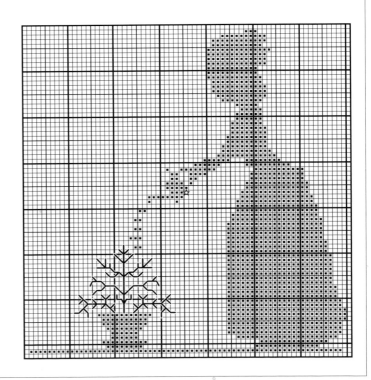

GRECIAN SILHOUETTE

This classical image of a woman dancing with a scarf, her hair blowing in the wind, appeared with a row of figures, some running, some hunting, on a Grecian vase. The early Greeks were very fond of using images in the form of silhouettes, usually black on gold, but often gold on black. The familiar and popular Greek key design is a classic example of this and has remained a favoured form of decoration throughout history.

DESIGN SIZE: 2¾ x 3¾ in (7 x 9.5cm)
STITCH COUNT: 64 x 86

Yellow 22-count petit point canvas, 7 x 8in
(18 x 20.5cm)
DMC stranded cotton (floss) black 310
Gilt cream – colour Versailles

Use two strands of stranded cotton (floss) over one thread of canvas.

In The Frame

This is one of my favourite designs from the book and much of the reason I like it in particular is the wonderful frame in which it is displayed. I am especially fond of black and gold, and so was more than pleased to find this ready-made delight with its beaded inner frame in the mount aperture. See Framing Your Work, pages 118–25, for advice on making a similar frame of your own. Incidentally, the card mount which originally came with the frame, was the wrong colour, so a black one was substituted.

1 To transform plain coloured canvas into gold background canvas, see step 1 for 'With Child' silhouette on page 70.

2 Find the centre of the design and work outwards from this point in tent stitch, following the chart. As tent stitch tends to distort the canvas, use a frame to keep your work straight.

3 Stretch, mount and frame as preferred (see Finishing Techniques, pages 116–17, and Framing Your Work, pages 118–25).

OTHER OPTIONS

∾ See 'With Child' Other Options, page 70, for an alternative gold background.

∾ Follow the example of the early Greeks and work the design in gold on a black background. Either choose black linen or dye a piece of canvas.

∾ Surround the design with a Greek key border (see chart on page 68).

Right: Grecian Silhouette (top) and 'With Child' (bottom).

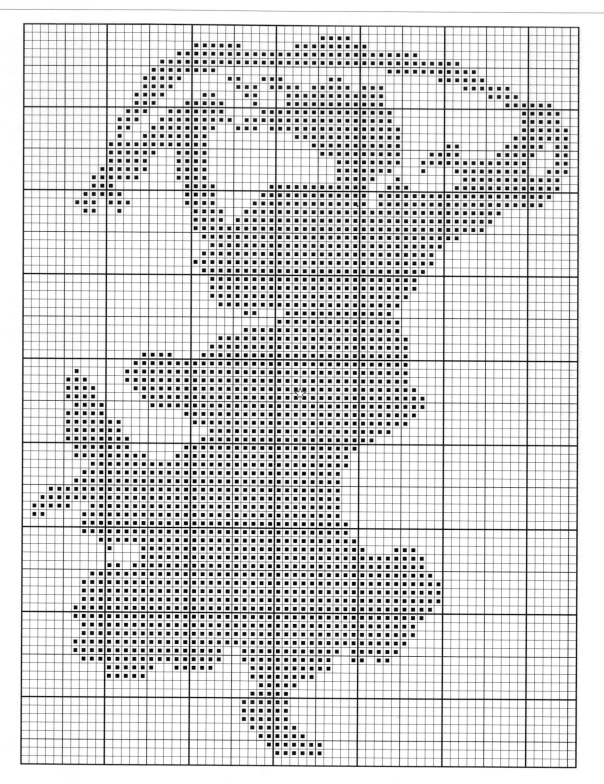

GRECIAN SILHOUETTE &
GREEK KEY PATTERN

DMC STRANDED COTTON (FLOSS)

■■ 310 black

☆ Middle point

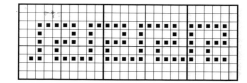

'WITH CHILD' SILHOUETTE

DMC Stranded cotton (floss)
■ ■ 310 black   ☆ Middle point

'WITH CHILD' SILHOUETTE

This is an alternative version of Matisse's 'Blue Nude' (the original was not with child). The striking stencil-like shapes of this figure (shown on page 67) with their wonderfully flowing, graceful lines and distinctive outline, make for a silhouette whose success lies in its simplicity.

DESIGN SIZE: 3 x 4¾ in (8 x 12cm)
STITCH COUNT: 68 x 96

Yellow 22-count petit point canvas, 7 x 9in (18 x 23cm)
DMC stranded cotton (floss), black 310
Gilt cream – colour Versailles

Use two strands of stranded cotton (floss) over one thread of canvas.

1 I created the gold-coloured background canvas from ordinary canvas and gilt cream. Lay the canvas on a sheet of newspaper. Apply the gilt cream with a stiff stencil brush using circular movements. Press quite hard and work in the cream, making sure that the canvas is well covered. Leave to dry.

2 Find the centre of the design and work outwards from this point in tent stitch, following the chart on page 69. As tent stitch tends to distort canvas, use a frame to keep your work straight.

3 Stretch, mount and frame as preferred (see Finishing Techniques, pages 116–17, and Framing Your Work, pages 118–25, for more advice).

OTHER OPTIONS

❧ Instead of colouring the canvas with gilt cream (if this makes you nervous!), you could fill in the background with DMC gold thread – see 'Mythical Bird', page 50.

❧ Work the design on a coloured linen. Frame using toning mounts.

In The Frame

ALTHOUGH THE SUBJECT MATTER for this design is more modern than the other silhouettes, I think the classic style of its frame suits it admirably. Very similar to the frame for 'Grecian Silhouette', but with a different coloured inner mount, this was another ready-made frame. It could accurately be described as 'a gift from the gods', so perfectly (but coincidentally) did it fit the subject matter. If you cannot find a ready-made frame that has an inner beaded frame in the mount aperture, make your own – instructions in Framing Your Work, pages 118–25.

GREAT OAKS FROM LITTLE ACORNS GROW

This design, based largely around the ever popular acorn motif, is adapted from part of a late 17th century sampler. The entire design, worked in backstitch on hand-dyed linen, is quick to work, great fun to do and makes a charming framed piece. When I was a child, I remember well my mother quoting, 'Great oaks, etc', on hearing me bemoan the fact that the scarf I always seemed to be knitting never appeared to grow!

**DMC STRANDED
COTTON (FLOSS)**
— Backstitch – 838
dark brown
☆ Middle point

DESIGN SIZE: 2 ¾ x 2 ¾ in (7 x 7cm)
STITCH COUNT: 40 x 38

Cream 28-count linen, dyed with Dylon's
  Koala Brown or a similar brown cold-water fabric
  dye (follow manufacturer's instructions), 6 x 6in
  (15 x 15cm)
DMC stranded cotton (floss) dark brown 838

Use one strand of stranded cotton (floss) over two
threads of linen.

1 Find the centre of the design and work
outwards from this point in backstitch,
following the chart.

2 Stretch, mount and frame as preferred
(see Finishing Techniques, pages 116–17,
and Framing Your Work, pages 118–25, for
more advice).

OTHER OPTIONS

❧ Use the design as it was originally, as part
of a sampler.

❧ Use the design to decorate a greetings
card.

In The Frame

A FRAME with a 'woody forest' sort of feel
was absolutely essential for this project;
and scorching a bought frame was the ideal
technique to achieve just that effect. It is
quite easy to do (see Framing Your Work, page
123) – and much more fun than buying one
that is ready-made.

FLOWER BASKETS

Flower baskets must surely have been one of the most popular subjects for
embroidery throughout history, and remain so today. Worked in almost
every technique from whitework to freestyle, at one time they also appeared in
the form of the beloved cardboard cut-out flower basket containing needles,
which could be found on sale in every good haberdashery department.
In the past they have decorated items as diverse as fire screens, cushions, tea
cosies, samplers and clothing. The following collection of flower basket
motif designs reflects this diversity by including a tradional-style sampler (shown
on page 74), a cushion and a small pincushion (both pictured on page 77).

THE SAMPLER

DESIGN SIZE: 5 x 3 ½ in (13 x 9cm)
STITCH COUNT: 130 x 77

Dark pink-brown (colour No 432) 25-count Lugana,
  9 x 8in (23 x 20cm)
DMC stranded cotton (floss) as shown in the key

Work in tent stitch, using two strands of stranded
cotton (floss) over one thread of fabric. As tent stitch
tends to distort fabric, use a frame to keep your work
straight.

1 Find the centre of the design by following the advice on page 17 and then begin to
work outwards from this point in tent stitch,
following the chart on page 75.

2 When the embroidery is complete,
stretch, mount and frame the finished piece
as preferred (see Finishing Techniques, pages
116–17, and Framing Your Work, pages
118–25, for more advice).

THE CUSHION

DESIGN SIZE: 8 x 8in (20 x 20cm)
STITCH COUNT: 83 x 83

White 10-count lockweave canvas, 12 x 12in (30.5 x
  30.5cm)
Dark green fabric for backing the cushion, 10 x 10in
  (25 x 25cm)
DMC Laine Colbert (tapestry wool) as shown in
  the key
Matching sewing thread
Terylene® filling
Twisted cord (bought or make your own – see page
  16) in a matching shade, 40in (102cm)

Work in tent stitch, using one strand of wool (yarn)
over one thread of canvas. Because tent stitch tends to
distort canvas, you may need to use a frame to keep
your work straight.

1 Find the centre of the design and begin to
work outwards from this point in tent stitch
following the chart on page 78.

In The Frame

THE FRAME FOR THIS PROJECT is one of my favourites, but when I first saw it, it was a monstrosity. Brand new, and only £3.99, it was a horrible, bright brass colour. I immediately went to work with my transformation kit: red oxide metal primer for a nice matt finish; when dry, Versailles colour gilt cream rubbed over the raised areas with a soft cloth; and hey presto a frame to be proud of. There are lots of frames like this one for sale, in many useful sizes. Do not be put off by the finish, you can alter virtually any frame you see.

FLOWER BASKETS SAMPLER

DMC STRANDED COTTON (FLOSS)

××	407 dark pink-beige
■■	951 very pale pink-beige
☆	Middle point

2 If the finished piece is not quite straight when completed, you will need to block (damp stretch) it (see Finishing Techniques, pages 116–17, for more advice).

3 Trim the canvas to within ½in (12mm) of the embroidery, cutting across the corners diagonally to within ¼in (6mm) to reduce bulk.

4 Pin and tack (baste) the embroidery and the backing fabric with right sides together, trimming backing fabric to size. Machine or hand stitch together, leaving a gap on the fourth side large enough for turning and stuffing. Oversew or zig-zag the seams to strengthen them.

5 Turn the cushion right sides out, stuff with the Terylene® filling, and close the gap with small invisible stitches.

6 Sew the twisted cord to the edge of the cushion where the embroidery meets the backing fabric, starting and ending at a corner. Make a knot at each corner, and when you reach the final one, tuck the ends under and stitch down firmly so that the cord does not unravel. (It helps to bind the ends of the cord with masking tape until they are stitched, this will prevent them from unravelling as you work.)

Left: The Flower Basket Cushion (bottom) and Pin Cushion (top) are both based on the Flower Basket sampler, showing that completely different looks can be achieved using different fabrics and threads. One of the baskets on the cushion does not appear on the sampler, but you could just as easily choose any of the baskets shown. The pin cushion uses just one of the baskets, and is surrounded with a green wool cord, knotted at the corners.

THE PIN CUSHION

DESIGN SIZE: 4 x 4in (10 x 10cm)
STITCH COUNT: 43 x 44

White 10-count lockweave canvas, 6 x 6in (15 x 15cm)
Dark green fabric for backing the cushion, 5 x 5in (12.5 x 12.5cm)
DMC Laine Colbert (tapestry wool) as shown in the key
Small amount of Terylene® filling
Matching sewing thread
Narrow twisted cord (bought, or make your own – see page 16) in a matching shade, 20in (51cm)

Work in tent stitch, using one strand of wool (yarn) over one thread of canvas. As tent stitch tends to distort canvas, use a frame to keep your work straight.

Just follow steps 1–6 of the instructions for making the cushion.

OTHER OPTIONS

❧ Make a larger cushion by adding more flower baskets (repeating the ones already shown).

❧ Use the design for a rug, working in cross stitch on rug canvas, and adding extra baskets until the rug is the size you want.

❧ Work the design in a different colourway, pale blues on a dark blue fabric for example. For a totally different look, try working the design in variegated or space-dyed thread.

❧ Using the waste canvas technique (see pages 14–15), work any of the individual baskets on items of household linen, for example napkins, sheets or pillowcases.

❧ Work just one of the flower baskets, chosen from the selection in the sampler chart and frame it as a miniature, or use it for a greetings card for a friend or relative.

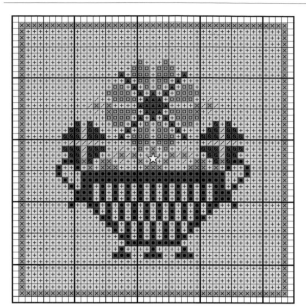

FLOWER BASKETS PIN CUSHION

DMC LAINE COLBERT

+ +	7141 beige	× ×	7370 mid green
⁄ ⁄	7853 very pale pink	▲ ▲	7226 mauve
● ●	7408 dark green	⊙ ⊙	7205 light plum
▭ ▭	7202 pale pink	☆	Middle point

FLOWER BASKETS CUSHION

DMC LAINE COLBERT

▮ ▮	7533 dark brown	▽ ▽	7429 very dark green
· ·	7141 beige	△ △	7335 grey-green
× ×	7313 pale blue	◤ ◤	7408 dark green
⁄ ⁄	7930 antique blue	↑ ↑	7370 mid green
⊙ ⊙	7205 light plum	● ●	7226 mauve
⊥ ⊥	7202 pale pink	☆	Middle point

TULIPS AND CARNATIONS

DMC STRANDED COTTON (FLOSS)

- ✕✕ 3773 pale pink-beige
- ■■ 356 dark apricot
- ▲▲ 951 very pale pink-beige
- ☆ Middle point

TULIPS AND CARNATIONS

This charming arrangement, worked in just three shades
is a perfect example of symmetrical simplicity. This piece was extremely
self-indulgent in that it was worked in the same colours we had chosen
for our newly decorated bedroom! This is an idea you could try yourself –
match the thread shades to the colours of your scheme, a DMC shade card
helps – substituting them for the three given here.

DESIGN SIZE: 3¾ x 4¼ in (9.5 x 10.5cm)
STITCH COUNT: 115 x 129

Cream 32-count Belfast linen, 8 x 8in (20 x 20cm)
DMC stranded cotton (floss) as shown in the key

Use one strand of stranded cotton (floss) over one
thread of linen.

1 Find the centre of the design and work
outwards from this point in cross stitch,
following the chart on page 79.

2 Stretch, mount and frame as preferred
(see Finishing Techniques, pages 116–17,
and Framing Your Work, pages 118–25, for
more advice).

OTHER OPTIONS

∾ Try working the design in shades of blue
or any other single colour (see 'Blue
Sampler', page 82).

∾ Work the tulips and vase design without
the border and make up as a pin cushion,
or use the design to make a pretty greetings
card.

∾ Work the design on a large mesh canvas in
wool (using tent stitch or cross stitch), and
make up as a cushion.

In The Frame

ANOTHER READY-MADE FRAME rescued from
its hideous print, this time transformed
by custom-cut mounts in toning colours. Most
picture framers will be happy to cut mounts
for you. You can, of course, do this yourself if
you are skilled, but I have found it to be a
very hit-and-miss affair (mainly miss!) with
frayed edges and a temper to match. So my
advice would be to leave this part to someone
with experience. After all, why spoil the
finished appearance of work you have taken a
great deal of time and trouble over for the
sake of a few pounds?

BLUE SAMPLER

There is something very satisfying about taking a single colour and exploring its possibilities within a design. Using one shade concentrates your mind on shape, content and symmetry in a way that a full palette of colours does not.

THE PICTURE

DESIGN SIZE: 6½in (16.5cm) diameter
STITCH COUNT: 101 x 98

White 32-count Belfast linen, 10 x 10in (25 x 25cm)
DMC stranded cotton (floss) as shown in the chart key on page 84.

Use two strands of stranded cotton (floss) over two threads of linen.

1 Find the centre of the design and work outwards from this point in cross stitch, following the chart on page 84.

2 Stretch, mount and frame the finished embroidery as preferred (see Finishing Techniques, pages 116–17, and Framing Your Work, pages 118–25 for further advice).

THE TRINKET POT LID

DESIGN SIZE: 3¼ in (8cm) diameter
STITCH COUNT: 101 x 98

White 32-count Belfast linen, 6 x 6in (15 x 15cm)
DMC stranded cotton (floss) as shown in the key
Cobalt blue porcelain trinket pot with a 4in (10cm) diameter lid (from Framecraft)

Use one strand of stranded cotton (floss) over one thread of linen.

1 Find the centre of the design and work outwards in cross stitch, following the chart.

2 Follow the manufacturer's instructions on how to fit the embroidery into the lid.

Right: The Blue Sampler Trinket Pot Lid (top) and Picture (bottom).

In The Frame

ONE PROJECT, two sizes, and two completely different ways of displaying it. The large sampler is framed with two circular toning blue mounts and a gold frame. A gold circular frame – beloved by the Victorian artisan – would be a wonderful alternative if you can find one that is just the right size. The smaller version is housed in a cobalt blue trinket pot. It's no happy accident that the colour matches the pot exactly, as the pot came first and the inspiration for its decoration later!

OTHER OPTIONS

∾ Following the example of toile de Jouy fabrics, try working the design in a different colour – subtle shades of pink for example. Toile de Jouy fabrics can also be seen in green and brown. If you have used one of these fabrics in your home, a picture or trinket pot lid worked in the same shade would be the perfect finishing touch.

∾ Use the design to decorate the lid of a round wooden (Shaker) box. This would make a perfect container for needlework.

∾ Use the design as a centre panel for a delicately pretty cushion with a frill of white lace.

∾ Work the smaller version as a miniature or make up as a pin cushion.

BLUE SAMPLER

DMC STRANDED COTTON (FLOSS)

■■ 336 very dark blue	▲▲ 930 dark grey-blue	✕✕ 932 pale grey-blue
▽▽ 3753 very pale blue	▪▪ 334 mid blue	☆ Middle point

ELIZABETHAN FLOWER

Of all the many motifs used in Elizabethan embroidery, the most loved and commonly worked was the flower. Two of the most widely used books of emblems, hugely popular in this period, were Claude Paradin's *Devises Heroiques*, (1557), and Geoffrey Whitney's *Choice of Emblemes* (1586). Both are positively overflowing with flower motifs in all their various forms, so it is not surprising to discover embroidered flowers on almost every item of clothing and household object made at the time. This flower is similar to one found on a spot motif sampler of the period.

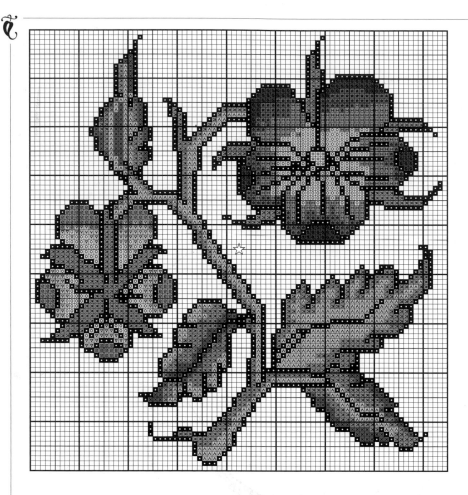

DMC STRANDED
COTTON (FLOSS)

◇ ◇   744 pale yellow
■ ■   310 black
▣ ▣   355 rust
H H   407 dark pink-beige
✦ ✦   356 light rust
∧ ∧   734 light sage
⊁ ⊁   731 dark sage
× ×   890 dark green
⩖ ⩖   224 dark pink
▽ ▽   950 pale pink-beige
◯ ◯   819 palest pink
☆   Middle point

DESIGN SIZE: 3 x 3¼ in (8 x 8.25cm)
STITCH COUNT: 83 x 88

Cream 28-count evenweave linen, 6 x 6in (15 x 15cm)
DMC stranded cotton (floss) as shown in the key

Work in tent stitch, using two strands of stranded cotton (floss) over one thread of linen. As tent stitch tends to distort the fabric, use a frame to keep your work straight.

1 Find the centre of the design and work outwards from this point in tent stitch, following the chart.

2 Stretch, mount and frame as preferred (see Finishing Techniques, pages 116–17, and Framing Your Work, pages 118–25, for more advice).

OTHER OPTIONS

❧ Surround the design with a floral border to make a charming miniature sampler.

❧ Use the motif to decorate the pocket of a blouse or other item of clothing, using waste canvas (see pages 14–15).

In The Frame

THIS HEAVY WOOD MOULDING was chosen not only because it complements the colours in the design, but because I felt it had an Elizabethan look to it. If you want to make the piece more modern, simply surround with toning mounts (circular, perhaps) and house in a simple gold frame.

ORANGE TREE

DMC STRANDED COTTON (FLOSS)

– – Blanc		⑤ ⑤ 727 pale yellow		⁄ ⁄ 733 light sage
▓ ▓ 3371 very dark brown		• • 841 dark beige		▲ ▲ 500 very dark green
▲ ▲ 402 light orange		▫ ▫ 921 dark rust		☆ Middle point

ORANGE TREE

The growing of orange trees has been hugely popular
in England for centuries. Conservatories owe their existence to the gardener's
need to cultivate and nurture plants and trees that were
difficult if not impossible to grow in our intemperate climate.
'Orangeries', as they were formerly called, were
built specifically for the cultivation of exotic and little known citrus fruits.

DESIGN SIZE: 4 x 5¼ in (10 x 13cm)
STITCH COUNT: 98 x 135

Yellow 22-count petit point canvas, 8 x 9in (20 x 23cm)
DMC stranded cotton (floss) as shown in the key

Work in tent stitch, using two strands of stranded cotton (floss) over one thread of canvas. As tent stitch tends to distort the canvas, use a frame to keep your work straight.

1 Find the centre of the design and work outwards from this point in tent stitch, following the chart.

2 Stretch, mount and frame as preferred (see Finishing Techniques, pages 116–17, and Framing Your Work, pages 118–25, for more advice).

OTHER OPTIONS

❧ Work the orange tree on a fine dark linen, such as 36-count unbleached Edinburgh linen, in cross stitch. This will give you a similar looking design without having to work the background.

❧ Work the design on a large mesh canvas in tapestry wool in cross stitch and make up as a cushion. Or you could use rug canvas, but use several lengths of wool (yarn) in your needle, to make a large wall hanging or floor cushion – either would be perfect for a conservatory.

❧ Use the design to cover a plain notebook, transforming it into a very smart gardener's diary – the perfect gift for a friend.

In The Frame

THIS IS THE SECOND FRAME I chose for this particular piece. The first was less chunky and, although nice enough, somehow did not have quite enough 'oomph'! Although it is a new frame, I found this one at an antiques fair – always a happy hunting ground for me. I usually find that antique dealers carefully choose new stock to blend in with their wares. This usually means a much better choice, and seems to ensure the quality of the new goods.

QUEEN ANNE HOUSE

This period of architecture, in my humble opinion, epitomizes English
house-building at its very best. Solidly built
in brick with precise and unerring symmetry, the house makes a
striking subject for canvaswork.

DESIGN SIZE: 7 x 5¼ in (18 x 13cm)
STITCH COUNT: 128 x 159

White 22-count petit point canvas, 11 x 9in (28 x
    23cm)
DMC stranded cotton (floss) as shown in the key

Work using three strands of stranded cotton (floss)
over one thread of canvas for the main body of the
design, which is worked in tent stitch, and three
strands over two threads of canvas for the background,
which is worked in satin stitch. As tent stitch tends to
distort canvas, use a frame to keep your work straight.

1 Find the centre of the design and work
outwards from this point following the
chart. With two strands of cotton (floss)
backstitch the top of the windows in 310
black. Work eight rows of background
surrounding the design.

2 Stretch, mount and frame as preferred
(see Finishing Techniques, pages 116–17,
and Framing Your Work, pages 118–25, for
more advice).

OTHER OPTIONS

∾ If you like the idea of stitching a house in
canvaswork but would prefer it to be your
own, see Charting Your Own Designs, pages
16–17, for more advice.

∾ Add your house name or number to the
design. The number could be worked in a
light-coloured thread on the door, and the
name either between the two chimneys or
underneath the house.

∾ Use the design as part of a large sampler
(as the stitch count for this design is 128 x
159, it would not fit into a smaller design).

In The Frame

I FELT THIS PROJECT needed a very simple
wooden frame. The subject matter is
straightforward, uncluttered and simple, and
needed a frame to match. If you are unsure
about framing, try describing your project to
yourself, and then buy a frame to match. This
method invariably works and will save much
soul searching at the framers. Although it is
wise to listen to advice, especially if you
are a novice, some framers are more used to
framing landscapes and photographs than
treasured embroideries; so read Framing Your
Work, pages 118–25, and remember that it is
almost always worth experimenting. After all,
if your frame and mount turn out to be a
disaster, you can always paint them!

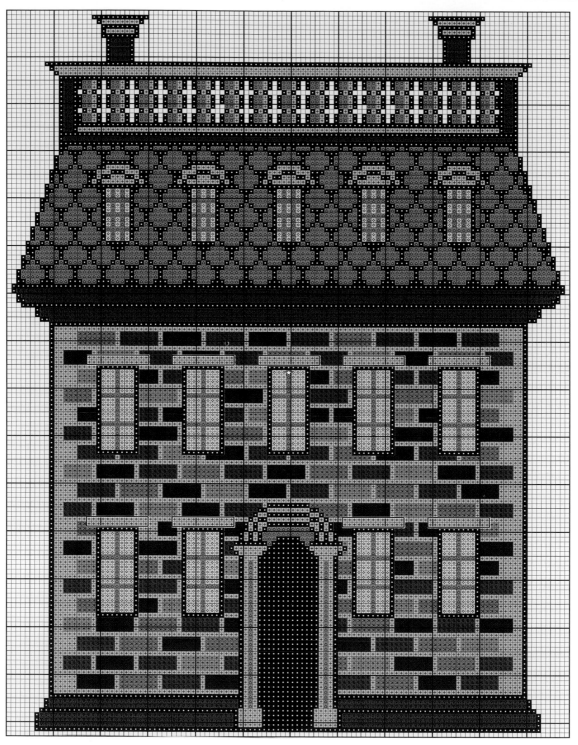

QUEEN ANNE HOUSE

DMC STRANDED COTTON (FLOSS)

- 310 black
- 781 mid tan
- 744 pale yellow
- 842 beige
- 926 grey-blue
- 918 dark rust
- 347 dull red
- 922 mid orange
- 642 grey-brown
- 902 maroon
- Background – 3823 pale cream. Work 8 rows of satin stitch over 2 threads of canvas surrounding the design.
- ☆ Middle point

DMC STRANDED COTTON (FLOSS)

- 3371 very dark brown
- 5 5 973 bright yellow
- ✕ ✕ 995 bright turquoise-blue
- ⋀ ⋀ 519 soft turquoise-blue
- 817 rich red
- ⊼ ⊼ 500 very dark green
- · · 745 soft yellow
- ▽ ▽ 730 dark sage green
- ⌐ ⌐ 733 light sage
- ☆ Middle point

BIRD OF PARADISE

The vibrant colours of this bird of paradise, set in
a wonderfully rich floral backdrop, make this a highly unusual piece. The
design has been adapted from a 16th-century Turkish (Isnik) tile. Isnik tiles
reached their zenith in the late 16th century and were acclaimed for the
dramatic quality of their rich colouring.

DESIGN SIZE: 4¾in (12cm) diameter
STITCH COUNT: 133 x 134

Cream 28-count evenweave linen, 8 x 8in (20.5 x
    20.5cm)
DMC stranded cotton (floss) as shown in the key

Work in tent stitch, using two strands of stranded
cotton (floss) over one thread of canvas. As tent stitch
tends to distort the fabric, use a frame to keep your
work straight.

1 Find the centre of the design and work
outwards from this point in tent stitch,
following the chart shown on page 93.

2 When you have completed the stitching,
stretch, mount and frame as preferred (refer

to Finishing Techniques on pages 116–17,
and Framing Your Work, pages 118–25, for
more advice and ideas).

OTHER OPTIONS

∾ If your eyesight is up to it, work the inner
design (without the scalloped border), over
one thread of very fine linen, 36-count
Edinburgh for example, and use to decorate
a trinket pot lid. A perfect base colour would
be the cobalt blue example shown in the
'Blue Sampler' project on page 82.

∾ Work the design on a large mesh canvas in
wool and make up as a cushion. If you wish
to increase the size of the cushion, simply
carry on working the background colour
until the desired size is reached.

In The Frame

THIS WONDERFUL GOLD FRAME shouts 'luxury' – unfortunately it had a price tag to
match. But I feel it's worth choosing the frame of your dreams once in a while. The
gold-coloured mount surrounding the embroidery was enhanced and given an aged feel
by rubbing a little brown varnish in a swirling motion over its surface followed by
Versailles gilt cream, lightly applied in the same way.

Miniature Samplers

These charming, traditional cross stitch samplers are an excellent example of how different the same design can look when approached in a different way. I worked the coloured version first and then, purely out of curiosity, the black one. I feel the black is the more successful. It seems to focus the design and concentrate the eye on the shapes and spaces around them. It's always interesting to see just how different a design can look with a change of fabric or thread, so try this idea with some of the other designs in the book.

COLOUR MINIATURE SAMPLER

DESIGN SIZE: 4¼ x 4¼ in (10.5 x 10.5cm)
STITCH COUNT: 103 x 103

25-count Floba fabric, 7 x 7in (18 x 18cm)
DMC stranded cotton (floss) as shown in the key

Work in cross stitch, using two strands of stranded cotton over one thread of fabric.

In The Frame

THE FLAT WALNUT FRAME that houses the coloured sampler is traditionally a favourite choice for samplers and is enjoying something of a revival. A set of decorative brass 'corners' used to be a popular embellishment , and you can still find these today; ask your framer for details. The black sampler is in a moulded wooden frame with matt grey-blue paint and an old gold finish – an easy effect to achieve on a plain frame (see page 122).

1 Find the centre of the design and work outwards from this point in cross stitch, following the chart.

2 Stretch and mount as preferred (see Finishing Techniques, pages 116–17, and Framing Your Work, pages 118–25).

BLACK MINIATURE SAMPLER

Design size: 3 x 3in (8 x 8cm)
Stitch count: 103 x 103

White 32-count Belfast linen, 6 x 6in (15 x 15cm)
DMC stranded cotton (floss) black 310

Work in cross stitch, using one strand of cotton over one thread of linen.

1 Find the centre of the design and work outwards from this point following the chart. Substitute your own initials using the letters on the chart and position as shown.

2 Stretch, mount and frame as preferred (see Finishing Techniques, pages 116–17, and Framing Your Work, pages 118–25, for more advice).

OTHER OPTIONS

❧ For a really homely sampler cushion, try working this design with wool in cross stitch over two threads of 12-gauge canvas. The finished size will then be 17 x 17in (43 x 43cm). Choose a neutral cream or light beige for the background colour.

❧ If your house has a name, you could personalize your sampler further by omitting the crown and substituting it with your house name. Use the alphabets given on this chart, working out your own details in pencil on graph paper (see Charting Names and Dates on page 16, for advice on positioning).

COLOUR MINIATURE SAMPLER

BLACK MINIATURE SAMPLER

DMC STRANDED COTTON (FLOSS)

3 3	738 gold-beige
◇ ◇	3766 soft turquoise-blue
↓ ↓	301 light chestnut brown

⊗ ⊗	924 antique blue
✕ ✕	371 light green-grey
▽ ▽	731 dark sage
⌊ ⌊	3371 very dark brown

■	310 black
☆	Middle point

Use the chart above and work the design in black thread only.

BARGELLO FLOWERS

DMC Medici wool (yarn)

- 8110 dark maroon
- 8418 mid grass green
- 8404 very dark green
- 8422 dark sage green
- 8124 darkest plum

Caron Watercolours

- 075 sunrise

DMC Stranded cotton (floss)

- 902 maroon
- 223 light plum-pink
- 225 pale pink
- 315 mid plum
- 3726 light mid plum
- 407 pink-beige
- 819 palest pink
- ☆ Middle point

Bargello Flowers

Bargello embroidery, also known as Florentine, Hungarian point or flame stitch, is characterized by wavy or flame-shaped stitch patterns. Named after the Bargello, or Podesta Palace, in Florence, it was brought to Italy in the 15th century by a Hungarian princess who married into the Medici family.

DESIGN SIZE: 5½ x 5½in (14 x 14cm)
STITCH COUNT: 124 x 124

White 22-count petit point canvas 9 x 9in
(23 x 23cm)
DMC crewel wool (Medici), stranded cotton (floss), flower thread and CARON Watercolours as shown in the key

Use two strands of crewel wool (yarn), three strands of stranded cotton (floss), two lengths of flower thread and one strand of CARON Watercolours. Work the tent stitch over one thread of canvas and the Bargello stitch over four threads.

1 Find the centre of the design and work outwards from this point following the chart on page 99. Consult the diagram below to work the corners using mitred bargello stitch. As tent stitch tends to distort canvas, use a frame to keep your work straight.

2 Stretch, mount and frame (see Finishing Techniques, pages 116–17, and Framing Your Work, pages 118–25, for more advice).

OTHER OPTIONS

❧ Try a different colour combination from the one shown. An easy way to blend colours successfully is to use a manufacturer's shade card, available from needlework shops.

❧ Use the design to make a centre panel in a cushion or, with a larger mesh canvas, simply carry on working the Bargello border outwards until the design is the required size.

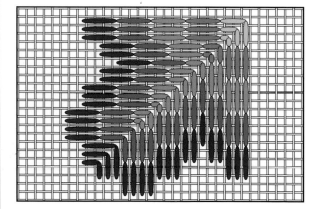

Four way bargello (or mitred bargello): diagram to show placement of stitches.

In The Frame

THIS frame, embellished with flowers, was the perfect choice for this floral-themed project. The colours of the mounts were carefully selected in order to complement the embroidery, and I chose simple muted colours so as not to detract from the design's own 'frame' of a Bargello border.

VICTORIAN FLOWERS

This tiny picture is an adaptation of one on a Victorian tile I bought many years ago, I thought it so pretty, I had it framed. The Victorians were extremely fond of decorative tiles. The artist William De Morgan produced some wonderful examples using brilliant colours and lustre, his hand-produced tiles are now much sought after. Although geometric patterns or flowers were the most popular form of decoration, such diverse subjects as Shakespearean characters, sporting figures, landscapes and even Aesops Fables have been used as decoration, and decorative tiles remain as popular today as ever.

DESIGN SIZE: 3¾ x 3¾ in (9.5 x 9.5cm)
STITCH COUNT: 95 x 95

Cream 25-count Dublin linen, 7 x 7in (18 x 18cm)
DMC stranded cotton (floss) as shown in the key

Work in tent stitch and backstitch, using two strands of stranded cotton (floss) over one thread of linen. As tent stitch tends to distort the fabric, use a frame to keep your work straight.

1 Find the centre of the design and work outwards from this point in tent stitch and backstitch, following the chart. Work the French knots last when all the other stitching has been completed.

2 Stretch, mount and frame as preferred (see Finishing Techniques, pages 116–17, and Framing Your Work, pages 118–25, for more advice).

OTHER OPTIONS

∾ This design would work very well as a cushion. Enlarge, by working on a large mesh canvas in wool.

In The Frame

SUCH EXUBERANT FLOWERS needed a strong coloured mount and an elaborate frame to do justice to their vibrant colours. I feel that projects of any kind – be they watercolours, photographs or embroideries – are too often finished with cream or beige mounting board. But with virtually every shade and hue available to us, why not use them? We have nothing to lose but mediocrity!

VICTORIAN FLOWERS

DMC STRANDED COTTON (FLOSS)

- 3024 light grey-beige
- 434 warm brown
- 676 gold
- Work French knots in 676 gold
- One strand 3813 soft turquoise and one strand 413 dark grey
- 3813 soft turquoise
- 919 mid rust

- 500 very dark green
- 413 dark grey
- One strand 730 dark sage green and one strand 3024 light grey-beige
- 730 dark sage green
- One strand 676 gold and one strand 413 dark grey

- One strand 315 dark plum and one strand 413 dark grey
- 315 dark plum
- One strand 3024 light grey-beige and one strand 315 dark plum
- Backstitch – 413 dark grey
- ☆ Middle point

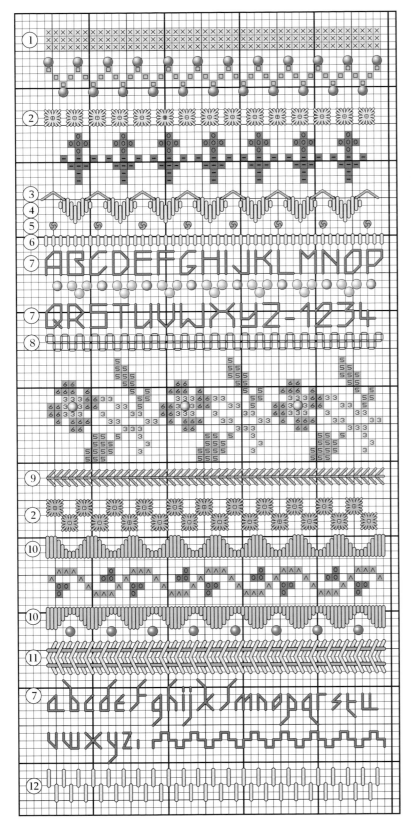

KEY TO STITCHES

1. Alternating cross stitch worked over 2 threads

2. Eyelet stitch worked over 4 threads (Ecru)

3. Backstitch worked over 2 vertical and 2 horizontal threads (927 pale grey-blue)

4. Satin stitch (Ecru)

5. French knots (754 very pale apricot)

6. Satin stitch worked over 2 horizontal threads and pulled tight (Ecru)

7. Backstitch worked over 2 threads (3063 soft pale-green)

8. 4-sided stitch (019 palest pink)

9. Backstitch worked over 2 threads (927 pale grey-blue)

10. Satin stitch (019 palest pink)

11. Diagonal satin stitch over 4 vertical and 1 horizontal thread with woven thread (Ecru and 754 pale apricot)

12. Satin stitch over 4 threads pulled tight (Ecru)

DMC STRANDED COTTON (FLOSS)

3 3	3770 very pale cream-pink
5 5	746 cream
6 6	754 very pale apricot
∧ ∧	927 pale grey-blue
- -	3053 soft pale green
× ×	Ecru
□ □	819 palest pink

MILL HILL BEADS

- 02010 silver
- 02016 soft turquoise
- 00146 pale blue
- 00145 pale pink

CARON COLLECTION

o o	Wildflower 054 pale blue

MINIATURE BAND SAMPLER

~

So delicate and pretty, this miniature band sampler uses a number of different stitches, threads and beads to add interest and variety. The 17th century band samplers were often a yard long and stored rolled on to a rod (often made of ivory), which was kept in a workbox and taken out when needed for inspiration for a further piece of embroidery.

~

DESIGN SIZE: 3 x 6 ¾ in (8 x 17cm)
STITCH COUNT: 45 x 103

Cream 32-count Belfast linen, 7 x 11in (18 x 28cm)
DMC stranded cotton (floss) as shown in the key
CARON Wildflowers pale lilac 064
Mill Hill beads as shown in the key
Beading needle

Use two strands of thread over two threads of fabric unless otherwise stated in the key. Use one strand of ecru stranded cotton to attach the beads.

1 Find the centre of the design and work outwards from this point following the chart on page 105 which gives detailed instructions for stitches and positioning beads.

2 Stretch, mount and frame as preferred (see Finishing Techniques, pages 116–17, and Framing Your Work, pages 118–125).

OTHER OPTIONS

~ Work only a 3in (8cm) square section of the design, from either the top or the bottom, and frame as a miniature.

~ Use the centre flower border to decorate napkins, towels etc.

~ Replace the bottom alphabet with your name and the date to personalize the sampler. Use the alphabet given, and work out your details in pencil on graph paper.

~ Make up as a miniature bell pull.

In The Frame

ORIGINALLY, band samplers were not framed at all, so there is no 'right' type of frame to choose. Antique band samplers that were framed at a later date are usually housed in plain wooden frames; but for this piece I chose a gold frame with a distressed finish. Try not to use very bright gold-coloured frames for samplers; bright gold will dominate and kill soft colours, and the effect will be disastrous. If you have a frame that is almost right, but the finish is too bright, try applying a little gilt cream to tone it down.

ASSISI BIRDS

Assisi embroidery originated in northern Italy, not in Assisi itself, but in the town of Burano near Venice. In 1870, nine years after the new state of Italy had been founded, a group of noble ladies took it upon themselves to revive the traditional handicrafts of the region. Taking their inspiration from religious artefacts, they simplified the images, working the outline in double running stitch and filling in the background with cross stitch. The background colours were the traditional red, blue, green or gold, with the outlines worked in black or brown.

For a more modern slant use space-dyed thread, which makes this Assisi design extremely easy to work as there are no changes of colour and only two stitches are used – cross stitch and backstitch.

DESIGN SIZE: 6 x 6in (15 x 15cm)
STITCH COUNT: 83 x 83

Cream 28-count Quaker Cloth, 10 x 10in (25 x 25cm)
CARON Wildflowers bark 016

Use one strand of thread over two threads of linen.

1 Find the centre of the design and work outwards from this point, following the chart. Work all the cross stitches first then add the backstitch.

2 Stretch, mount and frame as preferred (see Finishing Techniques, pages 116–17, and Framing Your Work, pages 118–25).

OTHER OPTIONS

∾ Try working the design in one of the traditional colours (described above).

∾ For a really luxurious look, work in black and gold thread. This could be used either as a picture (see alternative project pictured opposite) or made up into an extravagant pin cushion, backed in velvet, edged in gold braid, and with tassels at each corner.

∾ Personalize the design by adding your initials (these will have to be fairly small so use the alphabet from 'Miniature Band Sampler', page 105). Position them in the heart at the very centre of the design.

∾ Make a truly unique gift by adding a person's name, date of birth, town where they live and any other relevant details, just outside the outer border surrounding the design. Use a tiny backstitch alphabet such as the alphabet from 'Miniature Band Sampler', page 105 (see Charting Names and Dates, page 16–17, for advice on perfect positioning).

Assisi Birds

Caron Wildflowers

×× 016 bark

— Backstitch – 016 bark

Black and Gold Assisi Birds

DMC Stranded cotton (floss)

×× 310 black

— Backstitch – 282 gold thread

Alternative finial for
black and gold version

— 310 black

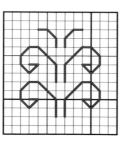

In The Frame

I THOUGHT IT WOULD BE FUN to follow
through the shape of this design for the
space-dyed version with the frame itself. As
the frame is very distinctive, I kept to pale
mounts so as not to swamp the design. For
the black and gold version I used mounts
to echo the shape and colour, within a dull
black frame with gold highlights. I painted
the inner mount over with gilt cream.

TULIPS AND
LAVENDER INITIALS

The tulip and lavender border surrounding this stylish initial is worked in subtle colours and has a rather Art Nouveau feel to it.

Work an initial as a gift for a friend: a personalized gift means so much more. Select an item to embroider from any of the ones suggested, or choose something to embellish which will have special significance to the recipient.

DESIGN SIZE: 4in (10cm) diameter
STITCH COUNT: 101 x 101

White 22-count petit point canvas, 7 x 7in (18 x 18cm)
DMC stranded cotton (floss) as shown in the key

Work in tent stitch, using two strands of stranded cotton (floss) over one thread of canvas. As tent stitch tends to distort the canvas, use a frame to keep your work straight.

In The Frame

THE FRAME for this project was a ready-made one I liked so much that I tailored the colours in the design to match – a method you might like to try, as it's so much easier to find a shade from DMC's range of 428 colours to match the frame than vice versa!

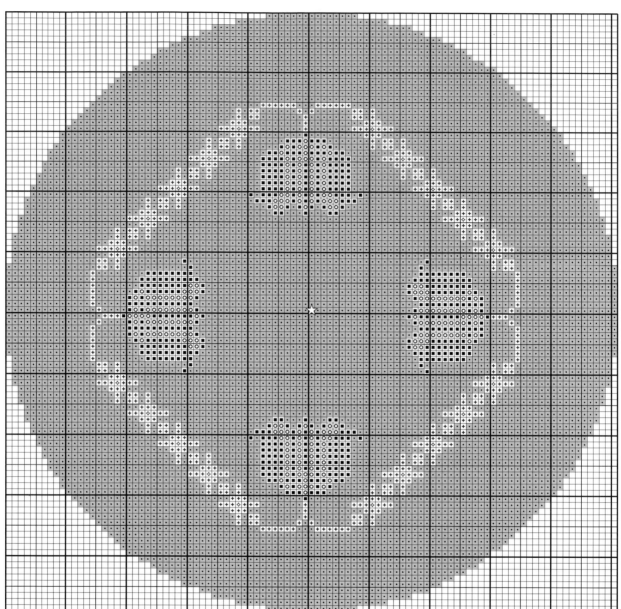

For key see chart opposite.

1 Find the centre of your chosen initial from the alphabet chart opposite and match to the centre of the main chart. Mark the position lightly on the chart in pencil (or a photocopy of the chart), then match to the centre of the fabric. Begin work at this point in tent stitch following the chart.

2 Stretch, mount and frame as preferred (see Finishing Techniques, pages 116–17, and Framing Your Work, pages 118–25, for more advice).

OTHER OPTIONS

꙯ Use to decorate a trinket pot lid.

꙯ Work the design on linen. Trim to a round shape and add lace around the edges to make a pretty dressing-table mat.

꙯ Using the waste canvas technique (see pages 14–15), decorate clothing or household linen such as napkins, pillowcases, sheets and towels with the initials.

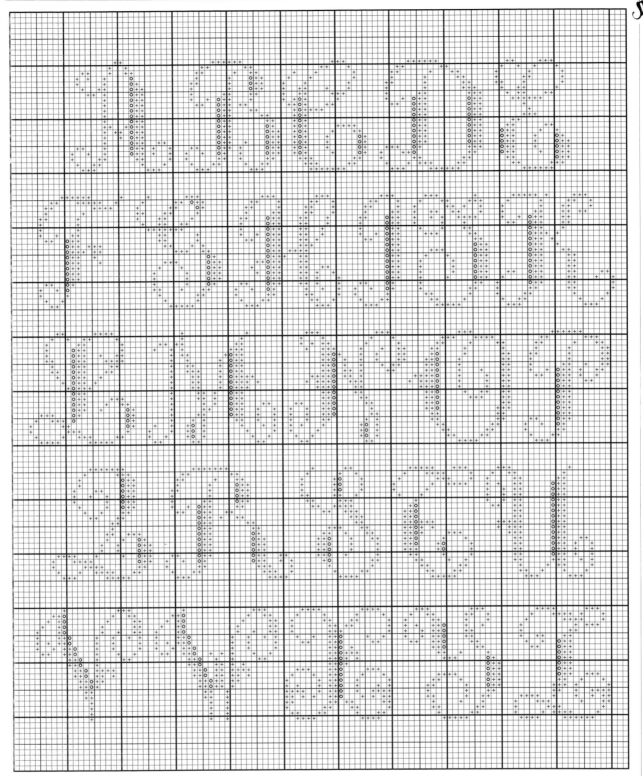

Tulip and Lavender Initials

DMC Stranded cotton (floss)

- ■ ■ 502 soft green-blue
- ◇ ◇ 356 apricot
- ○ ○ 407 pink-beige
- + + 951 very pale pink-beige
- · · 500 very dark green
- ☆ Middle point of chart on page 112

WHITEWORK INITIAL

Wonderfully luxurious, romantic and pretty, this delicately worked whitework initial adorns the lid of an exquisite cut-glass trinket pot – making the perfect addition to a dressing table in a traditionally-styled bedroom.

DESIGN SIZE: 2¾ in (7cm) diameter
STITCH COUNT: 87 x 87

White 32-count Belfast linen, 7 x 7in (18 x 18cm)
Threads as shown in the key
Cut-glass trinket pot with 4in (10cm) lid

The main body of the design is worked in tent stitch, using one strand of Marlitt or flower thread over one thread of linen (use silver thread as it comes). The backstitch surrounding the initial is worked with just one strand of silver thread – this is very fine, so use short lengths. As tent stitch tends to distort the fabric, use a frame to keep your work straight; a 4in (10cm) hoop is ideal for this project.

In The Frame

THE FIRST CHOICE to house this design *had* to be an exquisite cut-glass trinket pot – but a fine alternative would be a square silver frame plus a mount with a circular aperture. You might be lucky enough to find an antique frame which needs only minor repairs. You can find gilt cream in silver as well as gold (see Suppliers, page 126) and this can be useful for disguising minor blemishes and improving the overall appearance of frames of this sort.

1 Find the centre of your chosen initial from the alphabet chart on page 113, and then match it to the centre of the main chart. Mark the position of the initial lightly on the main chart in pencil (you may wish to make a photocopy first). Find the centre of the fabric by following the instructions on page 17 and match this point to the centre of the charted design. Begin working in tent stitch and backstitch at this point and follow the chart opposite.

2 When the embroidery is complete, fit it into the trinket pot lid, following the instructions given by the manufacturer (these will come with the trinket pot).

WHITEWORK INITIAL

- ■ ■ DMC D283 silver thread
- – – Marlitt thread 1012 light cream (outline initial with one strand of silver thread)

- △ △ DMC Flower thread ecru
- ▲ ▲ Marlitt thread 1212 very light cream
- ☆ Middle point

OTHER OPTIONS

❧ Work the design over two threads of linen in cross stitch (this will double the size), trim the linen to a circle, allowing 1in (2.5cm) around the design, and trim with lace to make a pretty dressing-table mat.

❧ Work in cross stitch, as left, on a much larger piece of linen and make up into a nightdress case trimmed with lace.

❧ Use the design for a pin cushion, either padded with a lace frill, or to cover a ready-made one with a wooden base.

FINISHING TECHNIQUES

Before taking your embroidery to the framers or framing it yourself, run through the following list:

❧ Check the completed design against the chart. It's so easy to miss out stitches, or even whole areas of the design.

❧ Turn your work over and check for loose, trailing threads. Check that the threads are secure, then snip off as close to the work as possible. Dark-coloured trailing threads in particular will show through light fabric and spoil the appearance of the finished work.

❧ If you have to launder your work, wash it gently by hand with mild soap flakes (or embroidery shampoo which is now available from needlework shops), taking great care not to rub or wring. Simply swish the embroidery about in the water. Rinse well, then roll in a clean white towel. Open out and leave to dry. To press, lay several layers of towelling on an ironing board. Lay the work face down on the towels, cover with a clean white cloth and press with a warm iron. This method prevents the stitches from becoming flattened. Do not iron canvas or perforated paper.

STRETCHING, BLOCKING AND MOUNTING YOUR WORK

This part of the finishing process is vital (unless your embroidery is very tiny indeed), as the most wonderful piece of work can be totally ruined if it is puckered or creased. It is a simple procedure to master, but if your work is to be professionally framed, your framer will be able to do this for you.

STRETCHING LINEN OR AIDA FABRIC

Strong acid-free mount board (available from good art shops), or
Hardboard (usually only for large pieces of work) covered with acid-free paper
Pins
Strong thread, such as crochet cotton
Needle

1 Measure your work and then cut the board slightly bigger than your embroidery if a mount is to be used or, if not, to the size of your chosen frame.

2 Place the card or covered hardboard on the wrong side of the embroidery and, when in position, secure with straight pins inserted

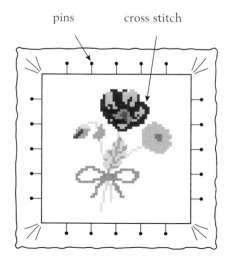

pins   cross stitch

Fig 1 Stretching linen or Aida fabric.

into the edge (Fig 1). Turn frequently to check that the embroidery remains correctly placed.

3 Fold over the side edges of the fabric, then use a long length of strong thread to lace back and forth (Fig 2a). Pull up the stitches to tighten and secure firmly.

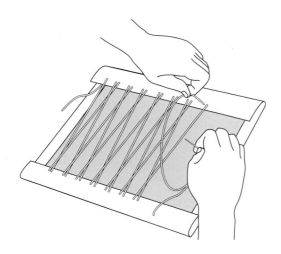

Fig 2a Lace in one direction first.

4 Complete the top and bottom sides in the same way (Fig 2b).

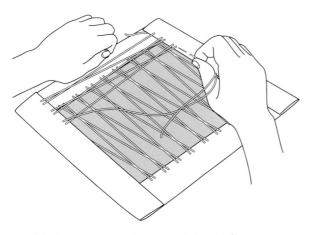

Fig 2b Lace across the remaining sides.

BLOCKING (OR STRETCHING) CANVASWORK

If you have not used a frame (or sometimes even if you have), canvaswork can become badly distorted and will need stretching back into shape.

A thick wooden board, larger than your embroidery and soft enough to take drawing pins or tacks
Several sheets of newspaper or blotting paper
Plain white porous paper on which you have drawn the outline size of your embroidery in waterproof pen
Brass drawing pins or tacks
For further materials needed for mounting your canvaswork, see the listing for Stretching Linen or Aida fabric opposite

1 Lay the sheets of paper on the wooden board and wet them thoroughly; a plant spray is ideal for this purpose. On top of this, lay the sheet of white paper with the size of your design marked on it.

2 Lay the embroidery right side up centrally on top of this. Then, starting at top centre, insert the drawing pins at intervals of approximately 1in (2.5cm), working outwards and stretching the canvas as you go. Pin along the bottom edge in the same way and then the sides (Fig 3).

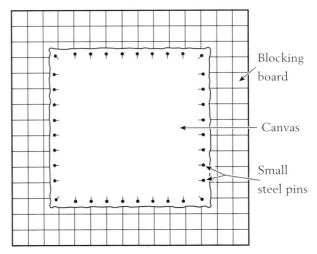

Fig 3 Place the embroidery on a wooden board and pin at regular interval.

3 Leave the canvas to dry thoroughly – this could take as long as two or three days. If the canvas was badly distorted, it may be necessary to repeat the whole process.

4 Lace the canvas over card or hardboard (depending on the size), following steps 3 and

FRAMING
YOUR WORK

It is vitally important to take your time when making decisions about framing – the frame can, quite simply, make or break a piece of work. However beautiful, unless you decide not to use a frame at all, your embroidery can only be viewed in its entirety together with its frame and therefore it's worth the extra effort to consider all the possibilities. A relatively simple piece of work can be greatly enhanced or even transformed with a carefully chosen frame and/or mount. You may have spent many hours on your work, so it would be sacrilege at this stage to spoil it. The first question to ask is whether you want to do all the framing and mounting, or take your work to a framer and get it done professionally. There are many skilled framers around, and they will do a good job. But don't be put off doing the framing yourself. If you approach the task with care you can achieve excellent results without going to great expense. It's also another opportunity for creativity. As well as advice on going to a framer, this chapter looks at choosing and covering mounts, transforming plain frames, even making your own.

MOUNTS

Almost any embroidered picture can be improved with the addition of one or two carefully chosen mounts, though the exceptions to this rule are samplers which were traditionally close framed. Firstly, let us consider cardboard mounts, with edges cut at a 45° angle to frame the work, not fabric-covered ones which are mentioned later in this chapter. No instructions are given for cutting your own card mounts, because I would very strongly advise against this. Just like plastering a wall, unless you are aiming for that 'rough-cast' look, leave it to the experts. I know it is possible to buy special tools for cutting mounts, but the old adage 'you get what you pay for' certainly applies here and the cheaper versions (in my humble opinion) are not worth the boxes they come in! Unless you intend to take up picture framing seriously, it simply isn't worth buying expensive equipment that you will seldom use. Mounts *always* look better if they are professionally cut, and any picture framer can cut the card at a 45° angle, and will be happy to do this for you.

A double mount invariably looks better than a single one and will add depth and interest to your work. Take your time choosing the colours as this is a vital part of the finishing process. An easy way to achieve success is to match the colours as closely as possible to those which appear in the design.

Consider using mounts with a shaped aperture. However, it is worth consulting your framer first: I once requested a heart-shaped mount and was presented with eleven rejected pieces of card with badly cut hearts, one unimpressive finished model, an exasperated framer (*not* the one I use now, I hasten to add), and a very large bill. Round, oval, triangular and similar shaped mounts should prove no problem, however, and there are framers around who specialize in extremely complicated and very beautifully cut mounts (see Suppliers list, page 126).

INNER-BEADED MOUNT

If you like the look of beading around the aperture of a mount (see 'With Child' on page 70, and 'Grecian Silhouette' on page 66), but can't find anything ready-made, it's not difficult to make your own.

Cut a mount with an aperture slightly oversize (or have one cut by a framer). Buy a length of narrow beading, cut lengths to fit the aperture, mitring the corners (you can buy a mitre board at all DIY outlets to help you to do this), glue together, and finish to match your chosen frame. Finally, apply a little glue to the outer edges of the beading and fit either inside the aperture or around the edge.

FABRIC-COVERED MOUNTS

By covering a mount with fabric you need not restrict yourself to a plain, uninteresting mount that does not do justice to your work. Virtually any colour, pattern or texture is possible with this method, and you could even add embroidery to match your design.

Strong card
Fabric
Glue or impact adhesive
Metal rule
Scalpel or craft knife
Cutting board or several layers of card to protect the surface you are working on
For a padded mount – one or two layers of Terylene® wadding (batting)

1 Measure the completed embroidery carefully and cut the mount and the aperture to the size required. Round, oval, and in particular heart-shaped apertures are very difficult to cut perfectly and, even though you are covering with fabric, uneven edges will show. Unless you are very skilled, it is best to ask your picture framer to cut these for you.

2 Cut the fabric to the size of the mount plus allowances for turnings. The allowance will vary according to the size of the mount and also the type of fabric (for example, velvet will require a larger allowance than fine cotton). Always make sure that you align the mount with the straight grain of the fabric.

3 Place the fabric right side down and position the mount in the middle. If making a padded mount, cut the padding to the same size as the mount and place between the fabric and the card. Snip off the corners of the fabric as shown by the dotted lines in Fig 1a.

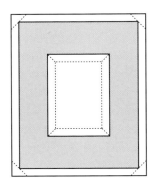

Fig 1a Position the mount over your fabric.

4 Apply adhesive to the remaining fabric at outer edge. Fold over and press flat.

5 To cut out the inside 'window', first cut out the rectangle as shown by the dotted lines in Fig 1a and carefully snip into the corners, stopping just short of the edge. Apply adhesive to this remaining fabric, fold over and press flat (Fig 1b).

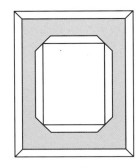

Fig 1b Fold back the inside edges of the fabric.

6 Apply any further embellishments you may like to add – bows, sequins, braids, etc – and then carefully align the mount over the embroidery. Fix with glue or masking tape.

Twenty Ways to Transform a Plain Wooden Frame

If you don't like what you see in the shops, the answer is simple: take what there is and transform it into something splendid! All the following ideas presume that you won't want to use glass with your frame. However, if you do, simply cut strips of wood (these don't have to be mitred) and fix by gluing and nailing, approximately ¼in (6mm) in from the aperture at the back of the frame.

1 Simple paint

Colour your frame to match either the project it will house or your décor. If you want a matt finish, use emulsion paint, but do bear in mind that it will be far more durable if you finish with two coats of matt varnish.

2 Straightforward varnish

Use traditional wood-coloured varnishes, such as oak, mahogany or rosewood; or, for a more modern look, one of the many primary-coloured varnishes. If you are even more adventurous, you could experiment on an old piece of wood with graining combs, feathers, sponges and the like. With practise, you will be able to achieve a number of different finishes that resemble expensive veneers. No specific instructions are given here as this would need a chapter on its own. If you are interested, it's worth asking at your library or bookshop for a book on the subject.

3 Fabric-wrapping

This is best with oval or round frames as it eliminates the problem of what to do with the corners. Cut several lengths of fabric on the bias, and join them together to form one long strip; how long depends on your frame. Make a small turning on one of the long edges of the fabric and press flat; then wrap around the frame, overlapping the fabric so that only the folded edge shows. If you want a more padded effect, wrap lengths of Terylene® wadding (batting) around your frame first. When the frame is completely covered, secure the fabric at the back with a few stitches, or glue into position.

4 Stuck-on pebbles or shells

This is very effective for an embroidery with a seaside theme. A flat frame is essential. Rather than go to the expense of buying something ready-made, all you need is a piece of MDF with an aperture. Shells are very popular at the moment, so look out for specialist shell shops which sell a wonderfully diverse selection. Use a strong adhesive to affix the shells to the wood as some can be quite heavy. If you're going to use paint, give the frame a couple of coats first as there may be gaps.

5 'Distressed' finish

For a wonderful finish you need just two colours of emulsion paint, a wax candle, a metal pan scrub and matt varnish. Paint your frame in the lighter colour. When dry, rub vigorously with the candle; don't cover the entire frame evenly, but do pay particular attention to the edges. Now paint all over with the darker shade, and when dry take the metal pan scrub and rub lightly over the surface of the frame – not too hard as you don't want to rub right through to bare wood. You will find that the areas that have been painted over wax will come away to show the colour underneath. Finally, finish with one or two coats of matt varnish for protection; since this is a distressed frame, however, you might feel this defeats the object!

6 Mirror mosaic

You will need a flat wooden frame, pieces of broken mirror, strong adhesive, putty and dark grey paint. Arrange the pieces of mirror all over the frame, and when you are happy with the composition, glue into place leaving a small gap between the pieces. Press small amounts of putty between the pieces (take

Right: A variety of different frames.

care not to cut yourself) and around the edges of the frame. When the putty is dry, paint it with dark grey paint so that it resembles leading.

7 STENCILS

Paint your frame first with emulsion, stencil in a contrasting colour or colours and then finish with a coat of matt varnish. Select the stencil to match the project – tiny bunches of grapes for a picture about fruit; stencilled letters for a nursery picture, and so on. Keep it simple and the frame will enhance, not swamp, your work. An alternative method that gives a similar finish is to use a potato stamp; make sure you leave the cut potato to dry out overnight, or the starch will fight with the paint.

8 STRING- OR RIBBON-WRAPPING

Choose string for a rustic look and coloured ribbon for a bright or pastel project. A flat frame is essential. Wrap the string or ribbon around the long lengths of the frame and secure at the back. Cut small, square pieces of wood the same width as your moulding, and either leave bare, varnish or paint. Glue the squares to the uncovered corners of the frame.

9 DÉCOUPAGE

Paint your frame with two coats of emulsion paint. Cut out suitable images from magazines, or photocopy images from copyright-free sources. Arrange them on your frame, and when you're happy with the composition, glue them into place. Finish with two or three coats of clear varnish. Black and white photocopies on a black or white painted frame look particularly effective.

10 SPLATTERED AND SPECKLED

Paint a frame in a pale colour with emulsion paint, then dip an old toothbrush in a darker shade. Flick the paint on to the frame (use lots of newspaper to protect surrounding areas) and finish with a coat of varnish.

11 GILT CREAM OVER PAINT

A wonderful method I have used many times in this book. A frame with a raised moulding is best for this treatment. First, paint with your chosen colour – black, red oxide, dark green and dark blue work very well. When dry, simply rub a little gilt cream over the raised area, and when it's dry buff to a shine or leave matt. Gilt cream comes in a variety of colours; a favourite of mine is 'Versailles', a lovely rich, old gold colour. It is extremely useful and versatile, and can be successfully used to disguise less than perfect frames. See Suppliers, page 126.

12 ORNATE OSTENTATION

If you have a plain, flat, cheap frame and wish it was a beautifully carved, intricate, expensive one, fear not, help is at hand. Many firms (Aristocast and Richard Burbage, for example) make wonderful mouldings that you can simply cut to shape and glue on to the surface of a flat frame. Cut the moulding with a mitre block and tenon saw, glue into place, sand any rough edges and fill in at the corners using a fine grade filler if necessary. Then just paint or varnish as required – and, as if by magic, a 'gallery' quality frame for very little expense.

13 MARBLED

Cut marbled wrapping paper with a craft knife to the size of your frame. A flat frame is essential. Smooth the frame with fine grade sandpaper, then paint with two coats of black emulsion paint. When dry, glue the paper to the top surface and use a roller to ensure perfect adhesion. When the glue is dry, finish with two coats of varnish.

14 ACCORDION FOLDS

These are simply wonderful with a brightly coloured, modern embroidery. Paint a flat frame with two coats of white emulsion. Cut strips of stiff white paper (a good quality paper is essential) the same width as the moulding, and fold like an accordion, joining strips with glue where necessary. When enough strips have been joined to cover the frame, apply a little impact adhesive to the back of the accordion folds, and glue to the painted frame, fanning out at the corners. Leave to dry.

15 BEAUTIFULLY BUTTONED

Transform a plain frame very easily with four beautiful buttons and a coat of emulsion paint. A small, flat frame is best so that your buttons don't look lost. Paint your frame in a shade that will enhance your buttons – black looks good with gold, primary colours with modern, brightly coloured buttons, and so on. If the buttons have shanks on the back, remove them with pliers. Then glue one button in each corner.

16 SPRAY-ON STONE

There are many wonderful faux finish paints (stone, granite, etc) on the market, and these are ideal for transforming plain picture frames very quickly and cheaply. They all come in easy-to-use spray cans in a range of colours that can be matched to your chosen subject. Follow manufacturer's instructions for use; these will vary according to your chosen finish.

17 WASHED-OUT DRIFTWOOD

Paint a frame in a pastel colour and then apply either liming wax (available from DIY shops; follow manufacturer's instructions), or a coat of watered-down white emulsion paint, remembering to wipe off the excess before it is dry. This type of finish works best on wood with a distinctive grain, such as oak.

18 BRAIDING

Adding braid can make a huge difference. Paint a frame in your chosen colour, then glue on the braid, mitring at the corners. The width of the braid will depend on how much of the frame you want to cover; and the style will depend on your embroidery. Brightly coloured ethnic braids would look wonderful with a plain black frame and would complement a modern design quite beautifully. Alternatively, disregard the colour of the braid entirely and concentrate more on its textural quality. Glue it to a bare frame and paint over all with a single colour (spray paints are ideal). This will add texture and interest to your frame, and you might even like to take this one step further and apply a little gilt cream to the raised areas.

19 FLOWERS AND FOLIAGE

Floral frames can be made very easily by winding wire around the frame and then affixing dried or silk flowers using small pieces of thin florist's wire. For a delicately pretty frame, surround a birth sampler with tiny rose-buds, colour-matched to the design; or make a rustic frame with twigs, dried fruit and flowers in autumn colours to surround an embroidery with a country theme. For a wonderfully extravagant Christmas frame, attach Poinsettia, holly, ivy and mistletoe to provide a stunning surround to an embroidered Christmas message. The variations for this type of frame are endless; simply use your imagination to create a unique finishing touch for your work.

20 SCORCHING

Take your frame outdoors, light your blowtorch and run the flame lightly over the surface until the finish is removed and the frame scorched and darkened. Clean the surface carefully so that no black, sooty bits get on to your work. This is a very simple technique, but potentially hazardous, so do take care.

MAKING YOUR OWN

Why stop at decorating bought frames? From the simple fold-over card to the fun lolly-stick frame, here are a few ideas to get you thinking about making it *all* your own work!

FOLD-OVER CARD

An enormous variety of ready-made fold-over cards are now available from art and needlework shops (see Suppliers, page 126). But if the size or colour you want is not available, make your own.

Thin card in a colour to match your design
Craft knife
Glue or double-sided sticky tape

1 Measure your embroidery to assess the size and shape of the aperture, but remember that round, oval and heart-shaped apertures are much more difficult to cut accurately unless you have great skill. Do not attempt to cut any aperture with scissors: always use a craft knife or scalpel.

2 Cut your card to the size and shape required (Fig 2a). Cut an aperture in the middle section 'B' and, using a craft knife, lightly score fold lines as indicated by the dotted lines.

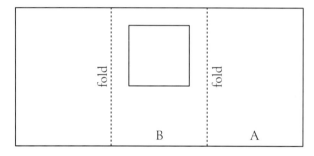

Fig 2a Cut your card to the required shape.

3 Position the aperture over your embroidery. Trim away any excess fabric and glue into position or secure with double-sided sticky tape.

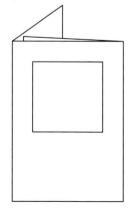

Fig 2b Fold and glue the sections in place.

4 Fold section 'A' over section 'B' and glue these firmly together (Fig 2b).

RUSTIC TWIG FRAME
A frame made of twigs or canes adds a charming rustic finish to a country-style embroidery.

Garden canes or straight twigs
Glue/impact adhesive
Varnish in a colour to suit your work
String

1 Stretch and mount your embroidery (see Finishing Techniques, page 116–17).

2 Cut garden canes, or straight twigs, to length. They will need to be about 1½ in (4cm) longer than the mounted embroidery.

3 Lightly glue them together, overlapping the corners.

4 Apply several coats of varnish in a suitable colour and then wrap the string around the corners of the frame so that they appear to be tied together (see the 'Exquisite Country' photograph on page 54 for guidance).

5 Finish with a string loop, glued to the back of the frame, for hanging.

6 Apply a little adhesive to the back of the frame and to the edge of your embroidery. Leave for a minute then press together. Cover the back of the work by lightly gluing a piece of paper round the edges and applying it to the back of the embroidery.

LOLLY STICK FRAME
Simple lolly sticks make an effective frame for a tiny piece of work. Buy them at craft shops or recycle your own!

Ice-lolly sticks, four per frame
Glue/impact adhesive
Paint or varnish in a colour to suit your work
Coloured paper for backing

1 Stretch and mount your embroidery (see Finishing Techniques, page 116–17).

2 Lay four ice-lolly sticks just over the edges of your work so that the corners cross (see photograph for 'Exquisite Country', page 54). When they are correctly aligned, apply a little adhesive to the point on each stick where the corners overlap. Leave for one minute then glue together.

3 Remove the design, then paint or varnish the frame on both sides and allow to dry. You may need more than one coat to achieve the desired effect.

4 Apply a little adhesive on the back of the frame and also to the outside edge of the mounted embroidery where the frame will be fitted. Leave for one minute then glue together.

5 Cut a piece of coloured paper slightly smaller than the mounted embroidery and glue to the back of the design.

AT THE FRAMERS

Whether you want your framer to do just part of the job – such as cutting mounts – or the whole thing, good advice will be offered about framing from a professional. But don't leave all the decisions to someone else; the creativity involved in presenting your work is just as much part of the project as stitching the embroidery.

I usually have a pretty good idea of the type of frame I want to use for a project before I have finished stitching it. Making your mind up in advance can, however, present problems at the framer's when you find:

a The type of moulding needed for this frame does not exist, or did exist but was discontinued yesterday;

b They have the moulding you want, plenty of it in many colours, but it looks disastrous next to your work;

c The moulding looks absolutely fabulous next to your work – but not in the opinion of the framer.

The thing to do now is take a deep breath, accept that you cannot have the exact frame you had wanted, and choose something similar; or go to a different framers and hope they stock what you have in mind; or buy a plain frame and give it your own chosen finish (see Twenty Ways to Transform a Plain Wooden Frame, page 120).

If you can, and I know this is not always possible to know in advance, go to a framer who is used to handling embroidery. Some embroidery shops do custom framing; you're more likely to find the kind of framer you want near an embroidery shop. Be prepared to disagree with the advice given, however; it's not like arguing with the plumber about which pipe he should use – this is art! Often, when you have lived with a piece for a long time, you get an instinctive feel for how it should look, so if you feel strongly about your decision, stick to your guns and if necessary go somewhere else. I have dealt happily with the same picture framers for years and they are by now used to my very often eccentric requests. Not so much as an eyebrow is raised when I ask for a 4in (10cm) wide moulding to be made into an 8in (20cm) frame – well, maybe a slight eyebrow twitch!

Unless your work has a very raised surface or is very textured, it's advisable to have glass in the frame as this will protect the work from dust, dirt and inquisitive fingers. Your framer will probably ask you to choose between plain or non-reflective glass. *Always* choose plain glass. Non-reflective glass certainly sounds the obvious choice but has a nasty, mottled, flat appearance which tends to dull colours. Plain glass will show your work to much better advantage. If you have decided to use glass but not a mount, ask your framer to use thin strips of card to prevent the glass coming into contact with your needlework. This will stop it from flattening your stitches.

SUPPLIERS

Canopia, PO Box 420, Uxbridge, Middlesex UB8 2GW – Wooden boxes for needlework

Craft Creations, 1–7 Harpers Yard, Ruskin Road, Tottenham, London N17 8NE – Greetings cards with pre-cut mounts

DMC Creative World, Pullman Road, Wigston, Leicester LE18 2DY – Zweigart fabrics and DMC threads

Falcon Art Supplies, Unit 7, Sedgley Park Trading Estate, George Street, Prestwich, Manchester M25 8WD – Framing

The Frame Workshop, 2 Old Market Place, Altrincham, Cheshire WA14 4NP – Specialist in framing art/hand-cut mounts

Framecraft Miniatures Ltd, 372–376 Summer Lane, Hockley, Birmingham B19 3QA – Trinket pots and Mill Hill Beads

Macleod Craft Marketing, West Yonderton, Warlock Road, Bridge of Weir, Renfrewshire PA11 3SR – For list of stockists of the CARON Collection

Siesta Bar Frames, PO Box 1759, Ringwood, Hants BH24 3XN

Silken Strands, 33 Linksway, Gatley, Cheadle, Cheshire SK8 4LA – Specialist shiny silk and metallic threads

GENERAL NEEDLECRAFT SUPPLIERS

With a mail order facility:

Campden Needlecraft, High Street, Chipping Campden, Gloucestershire GL55 6AG

Voirrey Embroidery, Brimstage Hall, Brimstage, Wirral, Cheshire L63 6JA

Wye Needlecraft, 2 Royal Oak Place, Matlock Street, Bakewell, Derbyshire DE45 1HD

When writing to any of the above suppliers, please include a stamped addressed envelope for your reply.

THE SAMPLER COMPANY

Brenda Keyes's sampler charts, complete kits and 'Country Yarns' Thread Organisers are available from selected needlecraft shops and also from The Sampler Company, Holly Tree House, Lichfield Drive, Prestwich, Manchester M25 OHX. Please write for details or telephone/fax 0161 773 9330.

BIBLIOGRAPHY

Bridgeman, Harriet, and Drury, Elizabeth, *Needlework*, Paddington Press Ltd (1978)

Butler, Anne, *The Batsford Encyclopaedia of Embroidery Stitches*, Batsford (1979)

Clabburn, Pamela, *The Needleworker's Dictionary*, Macmillan (1976)

Colby, Averil, *Samplers*, Batsford (1964)

Gombrich, E.H., *The Story of Art*, Phaidon Press Ltd (1950)

Gostelow, Mary, *Embroidery*, Marshall Cavendish (1977)

Grohmann, Will, *Klee*, Thames and Hudson Ltd (1987)

Huish, Marcus, *Samplers and Tapestry Embroideries*, Dover (1970)

Jones, Owen, *The Grammar of Ornament*, Messrs Day and Son, London (1856)

Keyes, Brenda, *The Sampler Motif Book*, David & Charles (1995)

Palumbo, Hayat, *Tapisserie, The Art of Needlepoint*, Weidenfeld and Nicolson (1991)

Pesel, Louisa F., *Historical Designs for Embroidery*, Dover (1970)

Rhodes, Mary, *Dictionary of Canvaswork Stitches*, Batsford (1980)

Snook Barbara, *English Embroidery*, Mills & Boon Ltd, London (1960)

Sutton, Ann, *British Craft Textiles*, Collins (1985)

Synge, Lanto, *The Royal School of Needlework Book of Needlework and Embroidery*, Wm Collins Sons & Co. Ltd (1986)

ACKNOWLEDGEMENTS

My grateful thanks to the following people for all their help and support:

My husband Chris, daughter Katie and son Nicholas for understanding why my creative energies are all used up on needlework, resulting in a pretty boring menu most of the time. (I can *decorate* a mean plate however!) My special thanks to Nick for producing most of the charts in this book especially as this was achieved in the midst of Martian Studies (or as they are more commonly known A-level Physics, Maths and Chemistry – all I can say is, I am glad I took up embroidery!) My mother-in-law, Irene and father-in-law, Jim for all their ongoing help and support.

My agent Doreen Montgomery for help, advice and very entertaining faxes. Everyone at David & Charles especially Cheryl Brown and Brenda Morrison. Jon Stewart for his exquisite photography and Barbara Stewart for her equally exquisite styling. Ethan Danielson for some of the charts and Mike Grey at Framecraft Miniatures for the beautiful trinket pots and Mill Hill beads.

INDEX

Page numbers in *italics* refer to photographs